York through the Eyes of the Artist

William Lodge (1649–1689)

'The Ancient and Loyall City of York'

Etching, 1678 (No. 1)

York through the Eyes of the Artist

Hugh Murray, Sarah Riddick and Richard Green

York City Art Gallery

City of York Leisure Services

ISBN 0 903281 10 4

Published by York City Council
for the exhibition of 4 August to 30 September 1990

Printed in Great Britain
by W. S. Maney and Son Limited
Hudson Road, Leeds LS9 7DL

Front cover
William Monkhouse
'York Minster As it appeared from St Peter's School, on the night of the Fire (May 20th 1840)'
(No. 103)

Back cover
Detail from Edmond Barker
'The South East Prospect of the Ancient City of York'
(No. 144)

Contents

Foreword

This publication records an exhibition of the same title shown at York City Art Gallery in August and September 1990. Consisting almost entirely of works from the Gallery's extensive topographical collection, it is by no means the first exhibition of its kind to be held here. Selections from the Gallery's collection of York views have been shown periodically over the years, the last major occasion being in 1981 when an exhibition *'the 2nd Citty of England'* was mounted. However, the present exhibition differs from all its predecessors in two important ways.

The first difference is that the exhibition has been recorded in permanent form in a catalogue which illustrates every item shown, many of them in colour. We hope this publication, of which more will be said below, will remain useful and attractive long after the exhibition has finished.

Secondly, nearly every work exhibited has been brought up to the highest standards of conservation, having been specially treated and remounted using correct acid-free materials. In this, the exhibition not only reflects the Gallery's continuing programme of remounting which has been underway for over a decade but more particularly embodies the work of a conservator of works on paper working here for the last three years. This temporary post was created in 1987 following consideration by the Council of a report on the state of conservation of the collection and with the proposed exhibition *York through the Eyes of the Artist* very much in mind. We were fortunate in finding an exceptionally capable conservator, Ruth Prosser, to fill it and almost every work in the exhibition bears witness to her skills. Sadly this intensive campaign of conservation has finished with the expiry of the contract and Ms Prosser is now a conservator with the Yorkshire and Humberside Museums Council. We hope it might be possible, however, to recreate the post at some stage in the future. In the meantime we offer our thanks to Ruth Prosser, without whose expertise the exhibition in its present form would not have been possible.

The nucleus of the Gallery's topographical collection is the large number of watercolours, drawings and prints amassed by Dr W. A. Evelyn and purchased by public subscription in 1931. Works had been acquired before this and the Gallery has continued to acquire works — by gift, bequest or purchase — since then. Although the Gallery is not in the market for topographical views simply because they depict York, in recent years we have purchased a number of York views where there was some particular interest in what was depicted or in the artist or in the aesthetic effect; several have been acquired because they complete sets or otherwise complement works already in the collection. Views in the exhibition by John White Abbott, Henry Gastineau, John Haynes, Thomas Rowlandson and Henry Rushbury illustrate this continuing policy.

The selection of the exhibits has not in fact been based on aesthetic criteria. Rather the views have been chosen for their topographical interest and to provide a cross-section of the collection. Nevertheless, the selection includes many works which will delight lovers of watercolours and prints for their own sakes.

A special feature of this catalogue lies in the topographical notes on each work. Lively, richly informative, often amusing, these have been written by local historian Hugh Murray, who has also provided an account of 'The Changing Face of York'. The selection of the exhibits has been the work of Sarah Riddick, Art Assistant at the Gallery, who has co-ordinated arrangements both for the exhibition and producing the catalogue; she has also compiled the artists' biographies. To Hugh Murray and Sarah Riddick, our grateful thanks are due.

Acknowledgement should be made of the financial support received over the years from the Yorkshire and Humberside Museums Council. This has greatly facilitated mounting and the establishment of the conservation studio. We should like to take this opportunity of thanking specially David Richardson of Gillygate Framing for his continuing and generous help with mounting and framing. Finally to everyone who has helped in any way with the exhibition and the catalogue, both within the Gallery and outside, we should like to record our appreciation.

We hope that both the exhibition and this catalogue will give great pleasure to our visitors.

Richard Green
Curator and Editor

York through the Eyes of the Artist

by Richard Green

The historic City of York, with its rich texture of medieval and Georgian buildings, might be thought by many to provide an obvious source of inspiration for the artist. It has indeed done so but only in comparatively recent times, that is to say since about 1650, and it was not until more than a century later that a solid topographical tradition was established.

Before the restoration of the monarchy in 1660 there was little taste for Gothic architecture and there was no appreciation of the irregular character of the City with its maze of twisting streets and crooked timber-framed houses. Celia Fiennes, that intrepid traveller on horseback, visited York in 1797. While admiring the Minster (for its size as much as anything), she thought that the City made 'but a meane appearance, the Streetes are narrow and not of any length, save one . . . the houses are very low and as indifferent as in any Country town, and the narrowness of the streetes makes it appear very mean . . . the buildings look no better than the outskirts off London'.

The City, she thought, looked 'better att the approach, because you see the towers off the gates and severall Churches in compassing the Minster and all the Windmills round the town, of which there are many'. Celia Fiennes had reached York from Tadcaster and William Lodge's etching '*The Ancient and Loyall City of York*' of 1678 (*Frontispiece*), the earliest work in this exhibition and a view taken from the south-west, corresponds closely with this description, even including a rare representation of one of the many windmills that were to be seen round York. Although the earliest known views of York date from the 1650s, the first substantial body of topographical work is associated with a group of amateurs, artists and antiquarians who came together in the City in the years 1670 to 1710 and were known as the York Virtuosi. Lodge, a gentleman amateur born into a prosperous Leeds family, was one of the group but the most important member, in the present context, was Francis Place (1647–1728). Born in Dinsdale, County Durham, Place was also a gentleman amateur. He had met Wenceslaus Hollar in London and in 1692 took rooms in the King's Manor. He made landscape drawings and also etchings and mezzotints, as well as experimenting in pottery. Many drawings resulted from sketching tours in Yorkshire and further afield. His views of York (such as Nos 57, 91, 115 and 119) reveal a curiosity about the subject depicted balanced by a restraint of execution. In these works we see the beginnings of an antiquarian interest which was to develop at an amazing rate throughout the eighteenth century.

Some of Place's drawings were used, after his death, to illustrate Francis Drake's great history of York, *Eboracum*, published in 1736. Another York artist, John Haynes (working 1728–55) was employed on this enterprise but Drake is likely to have experienced some difficulty in finding artists with the necessary skills to illustrate his work. Certainly for the engraving of the plates he had to resort to London printmakers. Nathan Drake (1727–1778), probably born in Lincoln, was one of the most active artists working in York in the third quarter of the eighteenth century. His painting of the New Terrace Walk which had been laid out along the bank of the Ouse in the years 1733 to 1740 was engraved by the London printmaker Charles Grignion. The resulting plate (No. 120) is the classic image of York as the fashionable resort for the county during the summer season which it had become by this time. But, however fashionable it might have been, there was not sufficient patronage within the City to support a local school of

Fig. 1

Michael Angelo Rooker (1743–1801) **Layerthorpe Bridge and Postern**

Oil, exhibited 1779 (York City Art Gallery, 900)

artists and it is symptomatic that this plate should have been engraved in London and not in York. Grignion has enormously improved on Drake's original, bringing a cosmopolitan grace and refinement to what would otherwise have been provincial work. Whether the New Terrace Walk — even at its most fashionable — ever looked quite like this is debatable! The Terrace Walk was one of a number of new attractions in York at this time, the others being the race course on the Knavesmire and the Assembly Rooms. These commanded the attention of the artist as did the new public buildings of more utilitarian use — the Debtors' Prison and Female Prison, the County Hospital and Bootham Park Asylum.

It was not until the 1790s, however, that a solid tradition of topography was established in York. By now, after more than a century of peace, which provided ample time for the contemplation of things other than day-to-day survival, there was an enormous interest on the part of the leisured classes in the history and antiquities of Britain, while more recently various theories had been published on the Picturesque. Ruins and crumbling buildings overgrown with vegetation, narrow twisting streets and half-timbered houses encrusted with the vestiges of age all became worthy of the attention of the public in general and the artist in particular. York could supply such subjects in ample measure.

Two York artists worked at the beginning of this period — roughly 1790 to 1850 — which was to be a golden age of the artist–topographer in York and also of the printmaker and print publisher in the City, for these activities went hand in hand.

Joseph Halfpenny (1748–1811) was born at Bishopthorpe, the eldest son of a gardener to the Archbishop of York. He worked in York as a draughtsman, etcher and drawing-master. His two sets of etchings, *Gothic Ornaments in the Cathedral Church of York*, published in twenty instalments between 1795 and 1800, and *Fragmenta Vetusta, or the Remains of ancient Buildings in York*, published 1807 (e.g. No. 62), are objective records of their subjects and, as such, key works in the antiquarian movement. Henry Cave (1779–1836) was a member of a well-known York family of printmakers and was a prominent drawing-master. He is perhaps best remembered for his folio of etchings *Picturesque Buildings in York* first published in York in 1810 and subsequently in London in 1813. These prints are important in being the first record of the fabric and texture of houses and other ordinary buildings, which are today valued so highly (e.g. Nos 15, 29, 75 and 83).

Robert Ledger (*c.* 1720–after 1763) had been the first printmaker to establish himself in York, setting up on the corner of Stonegate by 1755. He was succeeded by a continuous line of engravers working in Stonegate through to the mid-nineteenth century. In the 1830s lithography arrived in York, and its most successful practitioner in the City was undoubtedly William Monkhouse (1813–1896). He formed a particularly fruitful partnership with Francis Bedford (1816–1894), collaborating on the latter's *Churches of York*, which appeared in 1843.

Throughout the eighteenth century and well into the nineteenth, a whole series of artists based in London and elsewhere visited York. The brothers Samuel and Nathaniel Buck had come in 1719/20 to make drawings for two of their famous panoramic prospects of towns and cities. William Marlow came to York in about 1763 and produced several views of the Old Ouse Bridge (*Fig. 5*). Michael Angelo Rooker followed in 1769 and subsequently made two paintings, one of Layerthorpe Bridge and Postern (*Fig. 1*) and another of St Mary's Abbey now at the Yale Center for British Art, New Haven. Moses Griffith, a self-taught Welsh artist in the service of the antiquarian Thomas Pennant passed through York with his master in 1777, making at least four views of the City (Nos 17, 46 and 107). Joseph Farington stopped here to make a drawing of the Old Ouse Bridge which is dated 1783 (No. 65). John White Abbott, an Exeter apothecary and serious amateur artist visited York on his only extended tour outside the West Country made in 1791. He carefully titled, dated and numbered the drawings he executed on this tour: numbers 1 to 4 were of York and dated 13 June 1791, and are all now at the City Art Gallery (Nos 19, 20 and 43). His view of the Ouse Bridge (*Fig. 4*) he also made into an etching.

One of the most interesting visitors to York was Thomas Rowlandson. A number of drawings by him, both at York City Art Gallery and elsewhere, are ostensibly of York subjects. Until recently, however, it was by no means certain that he actually visited the City as the amount of accurate detail in his views was extremely limited and for one (No. 6) he relied heavily on Cave's etched views published in *Picturesque Buildings*

of York. However, the recent appearance of two pages of a sketchbook bearing an unfinished drawing of St Mary's Abbey suggests that he almost certainly did come here, probably in about 1800 (No. 36).

The artists of the Romantic generation — Turner, Girtin and Cotman — all visited York round about 1800. Girtin and Cotman both made watercolour views of the Old Ouse Bridge and Turner recorded it in a sketchbook drawing. However, the interest of York was Picturesque rather then Romantic. There was not really enough drama in the City or its setting to fire the Romantic imagination, compared for example with Durham where the cathedral is perched atop a precipitous cliff. It is perhaps therefore not surprising to find that Turner made only one 'finished' view of the City — a distant view of the Minster at dawn from the River Ouse, perhaps at Clifton Ings (*Fig. 2*). Henry Gastineau painted his watercolour *View on the Ouse near York* in 1826 (No. 64), having presumably visited York just before. This dramatic moonlit view, an exceptionally striking one for a pedestrian artist, might also be said to interpret the City in Romantic terms.

Over the centuries, artists have favoured certain views of York and have concentrated on certain buildings. The Minster has been constantly depicted since 1656 when Daniel King made several diagrammatic views. The parish churches have been well covered as have the defences, although interestingly it was only

Fig. 2
J. M. W. Turner (1775–1851)
York from the River Ouse

Watercolour, *c.* 1815 (private collection)

Fig. 3
William Etty (1787–1849)
Monk Bar

Oil, *c.* 1838 (York City Art Gallery, 64)

when the walls and bars were under threat in the 1820s and 1830s that they received the attention of the artist. William Etty the York-born painter was one of the leading voices in the campaign to save the defences and his interest is nicely documented by an oil painting of Monk Bar now in the City Art Gallery (*Fig. 3*). Painted probably in 1838 it shows the bar already bereft of its barbican, which had been lost in 1825; views of the inside and outside of Walmgate Bar and of Micklegate Bar by Etty are also recorded.

The Old Ouse Bridge was a constant source of inspiration to artists until its demolition in 1810–20. It was the single feature, apart from the Minster, which attracted the attention of visiting artists from Marlow, Farington and Abbott to Turner, Girtin, Cotman and Varley. It was also recorded by Halfpenny and Cave. With its pointed arch and buildings huddled at each end it clearly fulfilled Picturesque requirements; indeed it might almost be said that it made a perfect composition without further arrangement on the part of the artist. Above all it was reminiscent of the Rialto Bridge in Venice: Mary Ann Hughes, a clergyman's wife, was 'sorely grieved' in 1824 to find the new Ouse Bridge 'replacing the old Rialto-looking one so familiar to me

Fig. 4

John White Abbott (1763–1851) **'Ouse Bridge at York from an Arch under the Town-Hall'**

Watercolour, 1791 (York City Art Gallery, R2695)

from prints'. The artist Edward Dayes had gone even further in 1803, writing that 'with the surrounding objects it composes a scene that would have delighted Canaletti, and rivals many of his finest Venetian views'. The painting of *c*. 1763 now at York City Art Gallery by William Marlow epitomizes attempts to see the Old Ouse Bridge through Canaletto's eyes.

The solid tradition of the artist–topographer came to a fairly abrupt end in about 1850. The cause of its demise was the invention of photography or 'foe-to-graphic-art' as it had been dubbed, which offered a cheaper, quicker and in many cases more accurate alternative to what could be achieved by drawing, painting or printmaking. The dramatic and startling impact that photography had is illustrated by the example of Francis Bedford who gave up working as a draughtsman and lithographer and actually became a photographer.

Fig. 5
William Marlow (1740–1813) **Old Ouse Bridge**
Oil, *c.* 1763 (York City Art Gallery, 176)

Views of York have continued to be made since that time but the period of concentrated activity on the part of artists was over. A number of local topographers worked in York at the end of the century — W. J. Boddy (1832–1911, No. 63) and George Fall (*c.* 1848–1925) amongst them. If their work now strikes us as being over-brightly, even gaudily coloured, this can be explained. Colour was still something the artist but not the photographer could offer until well into the twentieth century when the commercial printing of colour photographs became viable.

Those in the first half of the twentieth century who recorded York very often seemed to be turning their backs on their own times and looking at the City through the eyes of earlier artists. Henry Rushbury is a case in point (Nos 34, 66, 129, 136 and 137). He was, however, an enormously gifted draughtsman and printmaker. Highly successful in its day, his work is once again beginning to receive the attention it once held.

In the years following the Second World War a very serious attempt was made on the part of the York City Art Gallery to bring its topographical collection up-to-

Fig. 6

L. S. Lowry (1887–1976) **Clifford's Tower**

Oil, 1953 (York City Art Gallery, 664)

date by commissioning each year a view of York from an artist of standing for the then considerable sum of fifty guineas. This scheme was named the Evelyn Award and it is through it that the Gallery came to have a striking and dramatic view of York from Clifford's Tower by John Piper (No. 134) and an idiosyncratic view of the Tower itself by L. S. Lowry (*Fig. 6*). The scheme operated from 1950 to 1962 when it foundered because it proved impossible to find artists of stature who were both willing and able to fulfil such a commission. It should be remembered that this was precisely the moment when abstract art was in the ascendancy within British art schools and the critical establishment. Nearly thirty years later the situation has changed. We now live in a pluralistic age when art of all kinds is produced and accepted. It might or might not be the time to consider relaunching the Evelyn Award scheme, if funds can be found.

Meanwhile shutters click thousands of times each day as tourists bring the City's sights within their camera frames. Wittingly or unwittingly they do this according to the dictates of an aesthetic that has a tradition of three centuries — from the measured views of Francis Place to the Neo-Romantic vision of John Piper.

The Changing Face of York

by Hugh Murray

York, over 1900 years old, is a 'continuing city', always adapting itself to the times, its character reflected in the streets, buildings and structures which remain from many periods of its history. From the arrival of the Roman Ninth Legion in AD 71 to the explosion of commercial developments in the closing years of the twentieth century the cityscape of York has gradually evolved round a street pattern laid down before the Norman Conquest. But at no stage of its development have the relics of previous ages been entirely swept away, although some, like those of the Vikings, have had to wait for recent archaeological excavations to reveal them. York is, then, a unique and largely unplanned collection of buildings of many periods in narrow medieval streets and the broader boulevards of more modern times. The whole adds up to a city that, despite sometimes calamitous restoration, is a wonderful place, loved by its inhabitants and a magnet for the countless tourists of all nationalities upon whom its future must depend.

The history of York, like Shakespeare's man, playing out his life on the world stage, has seven identifiable ages. From the first there remain the monuments of the Romans, who, having established their fortress in a defensive position in the fork between two rivers, surrounded it by a rampart of turf and clay topped with a timber palisade. Early in the second century these defences were rebuilt in stone, only to be rebuilt a hundred years later and then again in the fourth century. The Multangular Tower and the walls in the Museum Gardens and a column from the fortress, re-erected in Deangate, stand as symbols of this age when York had a prominent place in world history.

On the opposite bank of the River Ouse a civil town of tradesmen, army suppliers and camp followers had sprung up on either side of the road from the Roman fortress leading to the south-west. This crossed the river on a bridge which was destroyed by severe flooding in the sixth century, two centuries after the departure of the Romans, and was then diverted to a ford, where Ouse Bridge now stands, producing the great curve in Micklegate. King Edwin of Northumbria, baptized in a small wooden church which was the precursor of the present Minster, had made York the capital of his kingdom while Paulinus, who had baptized him, made it the ecclesiastical capital of the northern province. The Vikings, who captured York in 866, established their commercial centre in the Coppergate area, where evidence of their houses and occupations has recently been brought to light. The positions of many of the City-centre churches were established during this second age.

Following the Conquest, William reached York in 1068 and built two castles on artificial mounds on each side of the Ouse. To improve the defences, the Normans then set fire to the houses surrounding them and destroyed much of the City. Phoenix-like, a new city grew from the ashes of the old. New stone defences enclosed the Roman and Viking areas and a new suburb round Walmgate. Within the walls or just outside were forty parish churches. The religious dominance of the City was stressed by the presence of the great abbey of St Mary's, founded in 1089, four friaries, a priory, a nunnery and several hospitals and almshouses as well as the Minster, rebuilt and enlarged several times. York, as capital of the North, had entered a period of economic prosperity. The nobility of the North built their great town houses here, the richer citizens built timber-framed houses (jettied out over the streets to gain space in an overcrowded city) and the merchants and tradesmen built their guild-halls. But by the sixteenth century York was in decline: the larger ships could no longer navigate the river and the textile industry had moved to the West Riding. Henry VIII brought this third age to an end when, needing more money to pay for his wars with the Scots, he turned his eyes on the wealth of the religious communities.

Life in the City was disrupted by the Dissolution of the Monasteries. These had been major employers as well as providing succour for the poor and sick. The abbey and friaries were demolished for their stone while the house of the abbot of St Mary's, renamed King's Manor, gained a new role as an office for the King's Council in the North and a residence for its Lord President, the King's representative and effective ruler of the North. The Council's function was to bring criminals to justice, to hear civil cases and enforce religious observance. Its officers built their huge mansions in or near the City — the Duke of Buckingham in Bishophill, Sir Arthur Ingram in the grounds of the Archbishop's Palace to the west of the Minster and Thomas Eymes at Heslington. The presence of the Council helped York to regain some of its old importance as a centre of trade and social life. The two halves of the City were linked by the medieval Ouse Bridge, given a large and spectacular central span after floodwater in 1564 had carried away the central pillar supporting two narrow arches. By the time of Charles I the river was silting up, the Council in the North was dissolved and civil war was imminent: a new age was about to begin.

After the restoration of the monarchy in 1660 York entered into an age of elegance, entertainment and culture. The King's Manor became a place where the sophisticated provincial society could meet — until it was replaced by Lord Burlington's Assembly Rooms in Blake Street. The predecessor of the Theatre Royal opened in 1744. Regular horse-racing, started on Clifton Ings in 1709, transferred in 1730 to the Knavesmire where a grandstand designed by John Carr was built in 1754. The law, medicine and the arts flourished. Small family businesses provided what little manufacturing there was while the largest group of workers was in domestic service in the large town houses that the wealthy were building in the City. The County Hospital and Bootham Park Hospital provided places where the infirmities of the body and the brain could be treated if not cured. As the eighteenth century ended, the City came to life only during race week and assize week which preceded it. Its fortunes were declining. Its races and assemblies had lost the prestige they had enjoyed in the previous century and it was no longer the fashionable social centre: improvements in roads and stage coaches allowed those who could afford it to reach London in twenty-four hours. York had to wait for the coming of the railways for its sixth age to dawn.

At the beginning of the nineteenth century York was no longer a northern metropolis and consequently there was less money for capital expenditure. The neglect of the Ouse navigation by the City authorities made the import of coal expensive, which in turn prevented the establishment of manufacturing industries. Commercial progress was hindered by the requirement that anybody wishing to trade in the City had to be a freeman. The Municipal Corporation Reform Act of 1835 removed the latter restriction and the opening of a railway line on 29 May 1839 to South Milford and eventually to Normanton, connecting York with the coalfields of the West Riding, brought a reduction in the price of coal. For the rest of the century the population rose steadily as the new and expanding industries, and the railway itself, attracted workers to a transformed City. Terraces of houses were built outside the walls to provide them with homes, old properties in the City centre were demolished to create a new, larger marketplace in Parliament Street where they could buy the necessities of life, and two new bridges enabled them to get more easily to their places of work. Many new buildings, reflecting the new prosperity, appeared. At the same time many older ones were sacrificed in the cause of progress as new streets, including St Leonard's Place, George Hudson Street, Duncombe Place,

Clifford Street and Deangate, were constructed to improve access to and passage through the City.

The seventh and present age started as the First World War ended. Within the City walls large numbers of people were still living in poverty and sub-standard houses. With the War over, the Corporation acted immediately to solve this problem and continue a process which had been started in the years 1852 to 1881 when the notorious Water Lanes were finally cleared. Between 1919 and 1939 nearly 2,000 houses were demolished and nearly 7,000 people were moved to Council houses in Tang Hall, Heworth, Acomb and Burton Stone Lane, built in the fields beyond the terraced streets. This development continued after the Second World War and, in the City centre, faceless slab-sided brick and concrete buildings sprang up in answer to commercial needs. To deal with modern traffic a ring road had been planned and partly built in the 1930s but was overtaken by the outward expansion of the City. After the defeat in 1972 of a disastrous plan for an inner ring road this problem was partially solved by the completion of the outer ring road. A very welcome pedestrian precinct has recently been created in the historic core but the debate to find a solution continues. Shopping has been made more pleasurable — if one can find what one wants in the tourist-orientated shops: for the staples of life one is being forced more and more to the out-of-town American-style shopping developments growing on the outer ring road. Conservation now has to be carefully balanced against commercial economics which demand large buildings of a size inappropriate for an historic city whose attractions are based on the small-scale, informal, and irregular styles of previous centuries.

To the tourist, York appears to be an unchanging city, living off the glories of its past, but the reality is much different. The pace of change, never absent at any stage in its history, accelerates. The words of William Etty, the York-born artist, when fighting an attempt in the early years of the last century to pull down the bar walls, are no less true today. He wrote to the citizens 'Beware how you destroy your antiquities, guard them with religious care. They are what give you a decided character and superiority over other provincial cities. You have lost much — take care of what remains'. If this warning is not heeded, then the seventh age of York will be its last and it will be condemned, like Shakespeare's man, to 'mere oblivion . . . sans everything'.

Explanation of Catalogue and Map

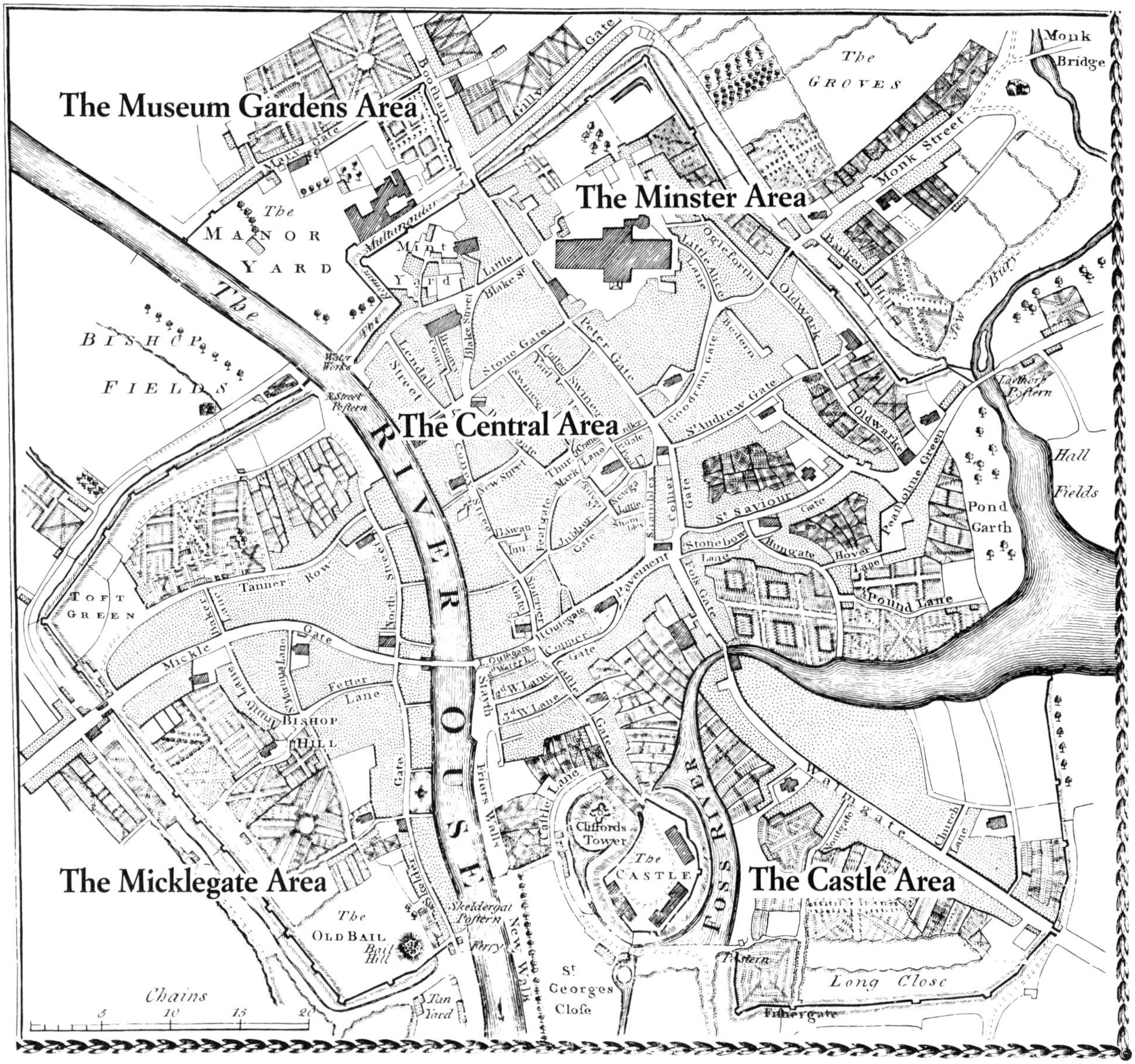

Detail from No. 10

The views of York in this catalogue are arranged within five geographical sections: the Micklegate area, the Museum Gardens area, the Central area, the Minster area, and the Castle area.

A relevant detail from the above map appears at the beginning of each section. Superimposed catalogue numbers indicate the approximate viewpoint of most of the works included.

Measurements are given height before width. Unless otherwise indicated, those for watercolours and drawings refer to the paper size and those for prints to the plate mark.

The Micklegate Area

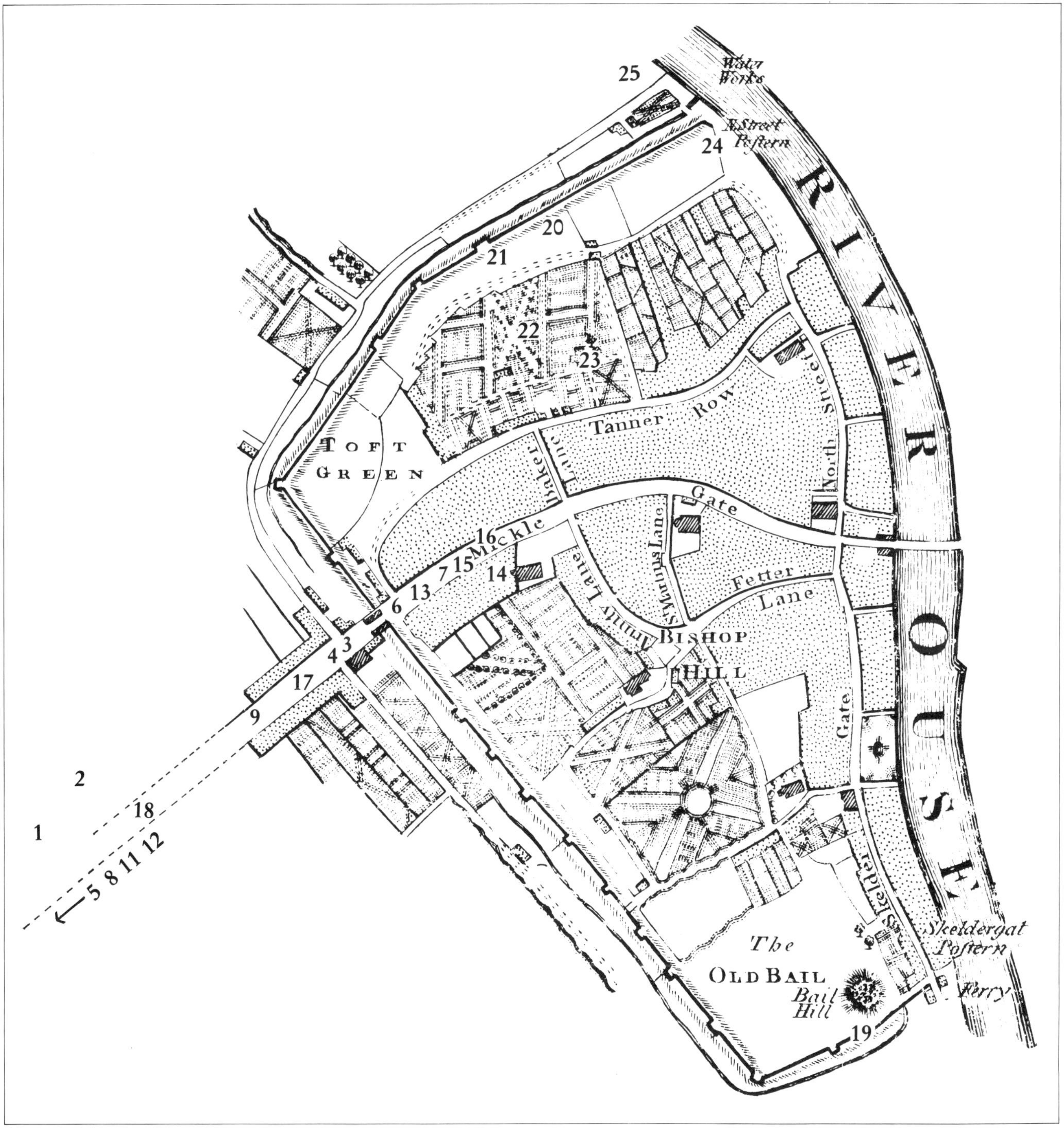

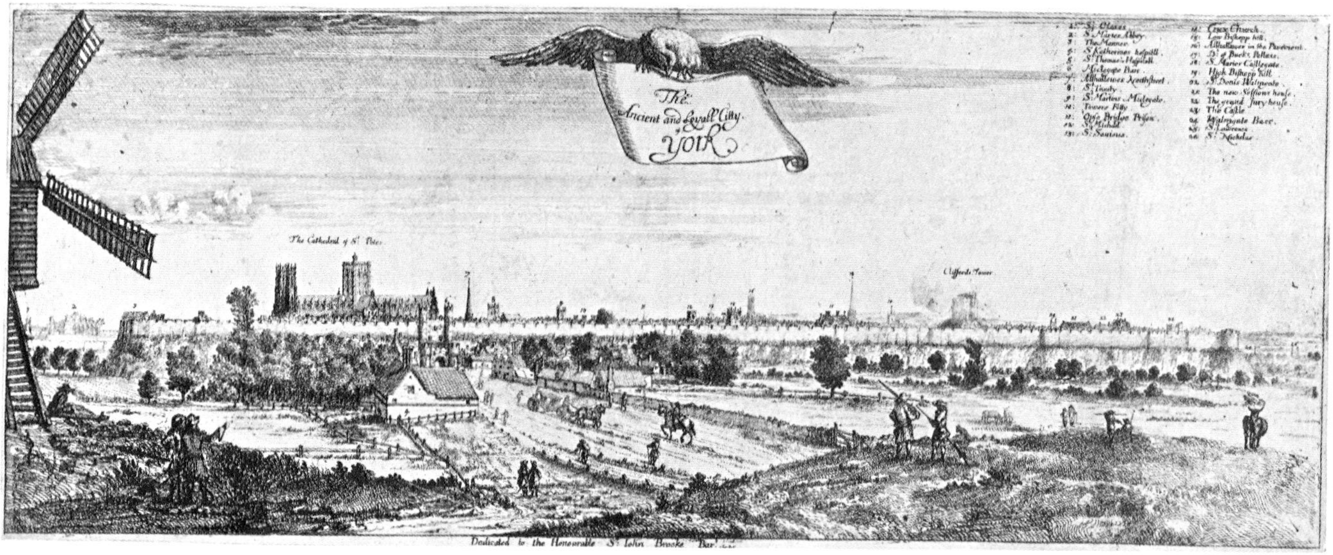

1

William Lodge

'The Ancient and Loyall City of York', *c.* 1678

Etching
7¼ × 18⅝ in (18.4 × 47.4 cm), image
Purchased as part of the Evelyn Collection, 1931 (R1988)

During the Civil War a gun emplacement was built by the Royalist defenders of the City on a platform on top of the small hill crossed by the road to Tadcaster, 'two great Bowshot from the Gate'. This ensured the survival of several old houses in Blossom Street which lay behind it. It is this hill or mount that gives the Mount, now a wide street, its name but in 1742 the City magistrates ordered that the mount be levelled and the high road 'which was before too strait [narrow] for Carriages, Coaches &c to pass and repass in that place', be widened. Before it was levelled the ruined fortification was a good place for artists to make their prospects of the City, with fields right up to the walls and the towers and spires of the churches silhouetted against the sky. The spire of St Martin-cum-Gregory had only just vanished, when this view was recorded, having been taken down in July 1677 and the tower topped with a balustrade.

2

John Harper

View at Holgate near York, 1830

Pencil
$10\frac{3}{4} \times 15$ in (27.3×37.9 cm)
Signed and dated 24 June 1830
Acquired by 1934 (R1694)

Since 1884 a part of the City of York and now struggling to preserve its identity, Holgate was once a small township, separated from the City by the Holgate Beck at the bottom of Holgate Hill. Just before the Boroughbridge road branched off from the Acomb road was a house which became the Crossed Keys Inn in 1776, its name a reminder that it then belonged to Dean and Chapter of York. By 1843 it had gained its present name, the Fox, which was transferred to a new building on the same site in 1878. The house in the angle between the two roads, leased by the Telfords from 1801 until the Backhouses took over in 1816, was sub-let to their nursery labourers until it was pulled down *c.* 1860. A similar fate had been suffered ten years earlier by the farmhouse opposite, last occupied by William Hebden.

A VIEW OF MICKLEGATE BAR YORK.
Published as the Act directs Jan.y 16, 1805, by Prince and Cattles, York.

3

Unidentified Artist

'A View of Micklegate Bar', published 1805

Engraving
$4\frac{1}{4} \times 7$ in (10.8×18 cm)
Published by Prince and Cattles, York, 15 January 1805
Purchased as part of the Evelyn Collection, 1931 (R2622)

Posts mark the narrow entrance into Queen Street, which was to be widened in 1907 to allow electric trams to reach the tramway centre at the railway station. This was achieved by pulling down the building which, by 1863, had replaced the one seen here next to the Windmill Hotel in the left foreground. Other posts prevent vehicles using John Carr's side arch created in an attempt to relieve the congestion caused by the barbican. Opposite the Windmill a rival, the Punchbowl, has appeared, replacing the inner range of St Thomas's Hospital. Punch became the fashionable drink at the end of the seventeenth century, being particularly favoured by Whigs to whom it signified change while, to the Tories, sack, claret and canary conveyed the values of the past. The punchbowl, then, became the sign of taverns patronized by the Whigs.

4

John Skinner Prout

Micklegate Bar, 1839

Pencil and bodycolour
11¼ × 9¼ in (28.5 × 23.2 cm)
Signed and dated 22 October 1839
Bequeathed by Dr P. A. Newton, 1987 (R3014)

Shorn of its barbican, Micklegate Bar, the principal entrance into the City, no longer has a convenient platform for the musicians who play the fanfares that greet the monarchs when they are met by the Lord Mayor on their visits to York. Now, on these occasions, scaffolding has to be erected for the trumpeters. The doorways that once led on to the parapet walks of the barbican, their doors now firmly secured, are a reminder of this fourteenth-century addition to the City's defences. When the bar was heightened in the third quarter of the fourteenth century to house the portcullis and its lifting windlass, its outer façade was decorated with the royal arms and two shields bearing the City's arms, one of the earliest appearances of this device.

5

Henry Cave

The Three-Legged Mare, *c.* 1800

Pencil
$5\frac{1}{2} \times 14\frac{3}{4}$ in (13.9 × 37.4 cm)
Purchased as part of the Evelyn Collection, 1931 (R1990)

On 31 March 1379 Edward Hewison was executed for rape on the new gallows at the Knavesmire. The York Tyburn, as it was called, was the place for hanging criminals from York Castle. Other authorities had scaffolds elsewhere: the Dean and Chapter had theirs in the Horse Fair at the end of Clarence Street, that of the Abbot of St Mary's was in Burton Stone Lane and the gallows of St Leonard's Hospital was on the Hull Road at Green Dykes. On execution days there were scenes of great callousness and rowdyism as crowds turn out to witness the punishment which, until at least 1745, included quartering. The Grand Jury decided in 1801 that the 'entrance to the town should no longer be annoyed by dragging criminals through the streets'. The new place for hangings was to be at the back of the Castle opposite the New Walk. After Edward Hughes was executed at the Tyburn, also for rape, on 29 August 1801 the 'Three-Legged Mare' stood disused, until it was removed in April 1812.

6

Thomas Rowlandson

Execution Day at York, (?)1820

Pencil, watercolour and pen and ink
7 × 10½ in (18 × 26.5 cm)
Signed and dated 1820
Purchased with the aid of a contribution from Sir William Worsley Bart, 1948 (R1707)

A tumbrel passes out of York through Micklegate Bar carrying three sorry-looking miscreants and their coffins to the place of execution at the Tyburn on the Knavesmire. Or does it? In fact the tumbrel is about to enter the City through a barbican. Whether or not the artist had visited York, it would appear that he was relying on etched views by Henry Cave which were published as *Antiquities of York* by R. Ackermann of London in 1813. Even though Cave had recorded Micklegate Bar (his plate 13), what is depicted here is Bootham Bar from outside the walls (Cave's plate 14), while the two buildings nearest the bar were in Low Ousegate (Cave's plate 4) and the other was part of the George Inn in Coney Street (Cave's plate 5). This fabrication was probably produced to commemorate one of two events — the last hanging at the Tyburn on 29 August 1801 or its removal in April 1812 after which all hangings took place at the Castle.

7

Thomas Rowlandson

York City during the Races, (?)1800

Pencil, watercolour and pen and ink
8½ × 11½ in (21.7 × 29.4 cm)
Signed and dated 1800
Presented by the York Civic Trust, 1957
(R1709)

On 16 August 1731 the regular race meetings which had started on Clifton Ings on 13 September 1709 were transferred to the Knavesmire. (This move was necessitated by the inundation of the course whenever the waters of the Ouse, swollen by heavy rains even in August, could no longer be contained within its banks.) With this transfer, Micklegate, on race days, became a scene of bustle and confusion. A young lady, visiting her aunt who lived in Bathurst House, recorded in her diary on 25 August 1812: 'we amused ourselves with seeing the Company pass in Coaches, Phaetons, Barouches, Post Chaises, Gigs and Dog Carts, besides a numerous train of horsemen and walkers.'

8

Unidentified Artist
with initials I.H.

York Races, 1769

Pencil, watercolour, bodycolour and pen and ink
$10^{3}/_{4} \times 13^{1}/_{2}$ in (27.4 × 34.3 cm), image
Signed (with initials) and dated 1769
Purchased, 1958 (R1802)

Not being able to join the nobility in the grandstand, the young lady mentioned under No. 7 watched three races from the field which 'was covered by spectators of all classes'. At the 1760 race meeting there had been only eleven races spread over six days in August but the spectators found plenty of other entertainment on their day out in the many side shows which had been assembled on the Knavesmire. These included 'A Main [match] of Cocks . . . fought between Mr. Thorpe and Mr. Lambert, consisting of 34 Main Battles, and 15 Byes; of which, Mr. Thorpe won 21 Main and 10 Byes.' In addition, on the Friday of Race Week 'The famous Mr. Johnson rode one mile for 100gs standing upright on horseback. He was allowed three minutes to ride it in, but performed it in 2 minutes and 42 seconds.'

9

John Storey
after Nathaniel Whittock

Bird's-Eye View of the City of York, 1858

Colour and coloured lithograph
21 × 36 in (51.2 × 91.5 cm), image
Printed by William Monkhouse, York
Published by Robert Sunter, 23 Stonegate, York
Purchased as part of the Evelyn Collection, 1931 (R1946)

The view-point chosen by Nathaniel Whittock for 'his splendid panoramic production', a point in the south-west several hundred feet above Blossom Street, has resulted in the area between Micklegate Bar and the river being portrayed in greater detail than the rest of the City. Micklegate curves violently away from its original alignment with a river crossing near the Guildhall which led to Stonegate and the Minster, the site of the Principia of the Roman fortress. George Hudson's York and North Midland Railway has penetrated the City's defences with two new arches through the walls to allow access to a station in Friary Gardens. On the other side of Micklegate a new street has been constructed to allow development of Trinity Gardens; this started in 1854 with Dewsbury Terrace, just inside the walls, and continued with the building by the Wesleyans of a chapel in 1856 and a school in 1858.

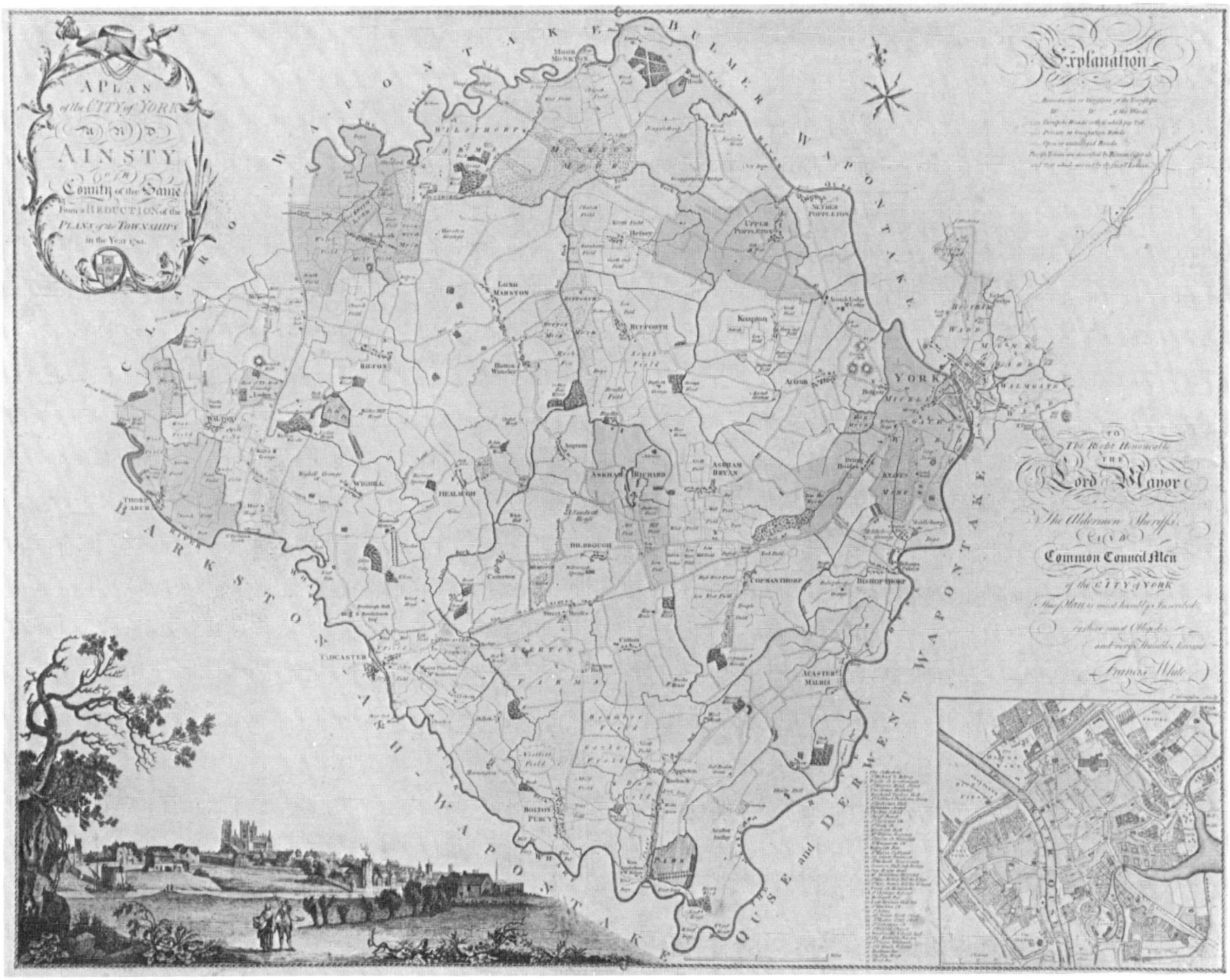

10

James Thompson
after Francis White

'A Plan of the City of York and Ainsty', 1785

Coloured etching
26¼ × 34 in (66.4 × 86 cm)
Dated 1785
Purchased as part of the Evelyn Collection, 1931 (R2738)

Until 1835 and the passing of the Corporation Reform Bill, York had jurisdicition over a large area on the west side of the City — the Wapentake (an administrative subdivision of a county) of Ainsty, containing thirty-five townships. The derivation of Ainsty is a little indirect. It is named for Ainsty Cliff, near Bilborough, which, in turn, takes its name from the Roman road which ran over the cliff. Originally Roman, by the time the cliff was named the road had deteriorated to a narrow path or *anstiga* in Old English. The City's boundary with the Ainsty, limited by the Ouse, was small, and all travellers from it had to enter the City through either Holgate or Dringhouses. When they reached the summit of Holgate Hill a panorama of York was spread out before them, from St Olave's church in the west, through St Mary's Abbey and its water tower, the Hospitium, the Minster, Lendal Tower, the Mansion House, to the spire of All Saints, North Street, in the east.

11

William Lindley

'A View of the Grand Stand and part of the Horse Course on Knavesmire near York', ***c.*** **1760**

Etching
$10\frac{1}{2} \times 15\frac{1}{2}$ in (26.8×39.2 cm)
Signed
Acquired by 1934 (R1774)

The young lady, who had watched the race crowds in Micklegate (see No. 7), went to the race course herself the next day, 26 August 1812, and was impressed with the grandstand, 'for which it is almost impossible to procure tickets being generally occupied by the nobility and engaged from one season to another' and which exhibited 'a variety of Taste and Fashion'. Dissatisfied with the amenities at the new course on the Knavesmire the Marquess of Rockingham, in 1853, had persuaded the race committee to open a public subscription for the erection of a grandstand. At least three designs were submitted and eventually John Carr's was chosen, and the new building was ready by August 1754, having cost £1,896. The ground floor had rooms for offices, entertainment and refreshment; a large room ran the length of the second floor opening on to a balcony for spectators who could also use the roof. When it was taken down in the early 1920s the lower storey only was rebuilt behind the present stands.

12

Thomas Rowlandson

York Races, (?)*c.* 1800

Pencil, watercolour and pen and ink
$9\frac{3}{4} \times 15\frac{1}{4}$ in (24.9 × 38.6 cm)
Purchased, 1954 (R1710)

The original race course on the Knavesmire, laid out and drained by John Telford, the nurseryman, was in the form of a giant horseshoe, nominally two miles long. From the starting line the horses raced to the opposite end of the horseshoe, round an 'exceedingly awkward and even dangerous turn' and returned to the starting line, now the finish, having covered the three miles seven furlongs and twenty-four yards. In 1845, when the Gimcrack Race was established, the course was made circular; the days of the long races were now over. The young lady mentioned elsewhere (see Nos 7, 8 and 11) recorded in her diary her impressions of a race on 26 August 1812. 'It is really astonishing to those who witness the scene for the first time to see the swiftness with which the contending animals fly over the ground. We were indeed gratified; and then to see the anxiety depicted in every countenance of the bystanders and the noise and bustle amongst them when the horses approach the winning post and the old women immediately ready to hand about the bills with the names of the horses and the colours of the riders.'

13

John Claude Nattes

Micklegate Bar from the City, *c.* 1800

Pencil and pen and ink
11¼ × 17¾ in (28.6 × 45 cm)
Purchased as part of the Evelyn Collection, 1931 (R2931)

In 1827 Peter Atkinson the younger designed a new stone façade for the interior of Micklegate Bar to replace an Elizabethan timber-framed structure, extending forward into Micklegate and similar to that still remaining at Walmgate Bar. The plasterwork of this extension was decorated with the City arms and above it were the royal arms with supporters and the inscription 'God Save the Queen'. The wall walk, which could be reached by a staircase at right angles to the walls, ran across the façade behind a battlemented parapet. All this gave way in 1827 to a duller, but historically respectable, uniform ashlar wall pierced on each floor by two square-topped windows, with the royal arms (introduced *c.* 1400) between the lower windows.

14

Francis Bedford

Trinity Priory Gateway, *c.* 1840

Pencil, watercolour and gum arabic with scratching-out
15 × 10¾ in (37.9 × 27.5 cm)
Purchased, 1934 (R11)

The gateway was the last vestige, apart from the nave walls of Holy Trinity Church, of the great Priory of Benedictines from the Abbey of St Martin of Marmoutier, near Tours. It had been divided into tenements, occupied by poor families who had no voice in the future of their homes which were 'ruthlessly demolished' with the destruction of 'a monument of the antient grandeur of our venerable city, . . . now to be reckoned among the things that have been and are not'. The newly-created Priory Street was to become one of the principal centres of Non-Conformity in York, providing places of worship for Wesleyans, Baptists and Presbyterians.

15

Henry Cave

'Portal to the Priory of St Trinity', 1813

Etching
10 × 7¾ in (25.5 × 20 cm)
Signed twice
Provenance unknown (R2263)

16

Henry Cave

'In Micklegate', 1830

Pencil
11 × 8¾ in (27.8 × 22 cm)
Acquired by 1934 (R2867)

The York and North Midland Railway's route to London was somewhat tortuous, passing through Normanton and Derby, and the journey took, at first, ten hours, although it was reduced, by 1848, to just over six hours. This could be further improved by a more direct route and, to the chagrin of George Hudson, a company was formed in 1844 to do just that. It proposed to build its station on the other side of Micklegate in Trinity Gardens. Opposition from the Corporation, led by Alderman Hudson, brought this scheme to nothing and Trinity Gardens were left undisturbed for another ten years until, in 1854, they were sold to a Mr Crawshaw for building development in the rapidly expanding Victorian City. Two schemes for the site were prepared by George Townsend Andrews; one, the more imaginative, had the access road branching round a central oval garden but it was the other, a simpler scheme, which was adopted. Both, however, required the demolition of the thirteenth-century priory gateway in Micklegate.

17

Moses Griffith

Micklegate Bar, 1777

Pencil, watercolour and pen and ink
$5^{3}/_{4} \times 7^{1}/_{2}$ in (14.5 × 18.9 cm), image
Signed
Purchased, 1913 (R373)

The fourteenth-century barbican on Micklegate Bar became an annoying hindrance to vehicles and pedestrians entering and leaving the City, which was not entirely alleviated by the provision of a side arch, designed by John Carr, in 1753. Following its partial collapse in 1810 the barbican was completely removed in 1826. On Nunnery Lane corner the twin-gabled building of St Thomas's Hospital was first reduced in size in 1787 leaving only the corner range which, in turn, was demolished in 1863 as its accommodation had been condemned as 'low, damp, the lower rooms especially ill-ventilated and dark with brick floors'. Its occupants, twelve poor widows, who until 1791 had to beg on the street four days a year for alms for their subsistence, were moved to a newly-built hospital (now the Moat Hotel) further down Nunnery Lane. In 1731 the house on the nearer corner was owned by a Mr Benson; it was later acquired by the Institute of the Blessed Virgin Mary who replaced it in 1844 by a Poor School.

18

William Monkhouse

Blossom Street looking towards Micklegate Bar, *c.* 1845

Coloured lithograph
$6^{1}/_{2} \times 9^{1}/_{2}$ in (16.4 × 24 cm)
Signed
Purchased as part of the Evelyn Collection, 1931 (R1776)

In 1845 the Punchbowl (just to the right of Micklegate Bar), which in recent years has spread sideways into most of the premises between the bar and Nunnery Lane, occupied only a part of a new building on the site. Nunnery Lane corner (further to the right) had very recently been graced by the giant Doric pilasters of the Poor School, designed by George Townsend Andrews, with a plinth which becomes an ideal vantage point on state occasions for the sisters of the Bar Convent, of which it was part. The foundress of their order, Mary Ward, was a pioneer of education for girls and in 1686 Mother Frances Bedingfield, the first Superior, bought a large house here to start a boarding school for young Catholic ladies. This house was replaced in 1786 by the generously proportioned seven-bayed building (seen here) with stone facings, the work of Thomas Atkinson. South Parade (leading off the right foreground), an elegant terrace of twenty houses built by the York Commercial Building Company between 1824 and 1828 for genteel occupiers, was nearly lost in more recent years when the Corporation decided that it 'was due for demolition by 1970 on health grounds'!

19

John White Abbott

'The Minster at York from the City Walls', 1791

Pencil, watercolour and pen and ink, on the artist's original wash-line mount
$9\frac{1}{2} \times 7\frac{1}{2}$ in (24.2×19 cm)
Signed and dated 13 June 1791 (on the reverse)
Purchased, 1947 (R2)

The Old Baile, on the west side of the river opposite Clifford's Tower, is also an artificial mound. Like its still fortified companion it was constructed by the Normans in 1068 and topped with a timber fort. By the fourteenth century it had passed into the hands of the archbishops of York who agreed to defend it in times of war provided that, if the Scots attacked, the City Guard would help in its defence. By the middle of the fifteenth century, after a dispute with the archbishops, the Old Baile passed into the possession of the City and was leased-out for grazing. It was last used defensively during the Civil War when two cannons were mounted on it and then, in 1726, 'this mount, the pleasantest place for the prospect about the city' was planted with trees by Henry Pawson, a merchant and tenant of the Old Baile. The trees now on the hill are the successors of the 1726 planting.

20

John White Abbott

'The Minster at York from the City Walls', 1791

Pencil, watercolour and pen and ink, on the artist's original wash-line mount
$7\frac{1}{2} \times 9\frac{1}{2}$ in (19 × 24.1 cm)
Signed and dated 13 June 1791 (on the reverse)
Purchased with the aid of grants from the Museums and Galleries Commission through the Victoria and Albert Museum, the Friends of York Art Gallery, Anthony Boynton-Wood, Esq., the Company of Merchants of the Staple of England, the Historic Houses Association Yorkshire Region and the Henry Vyner Charitable Trust, 1987 (R3024)

In 1736 Francis Drake in *Eboracum* recorded that the site of the Dominican Friary at Toft Green was then in the possession of 'Mr. Tilford, a worthy citizen, and whose knowledge in the mystery of gardening renders him of credit to his profession; being one of the first that brought our northern gentry into the method of planting and raising all kinds of forest trees, for use and ornament'. George Telford took his freedom of the City in 1684 and from that time his family went on to establish a considerable reputation as nurserymen before, in 1816, selling the nursery in Friary Gardens to Thomas and James Backhouse, Quakers from Darlington. From 1700 a house in the gardens had been occupied by Lady Hewley's Hospital and in 1814 a prison was built at the southern end for malefactors from the Ainsty.

21

Michael Ayrton

York from the Walls, 1951 (with preliminary sketch on the reverse)

Pencil, bodycolour, pen and black ink, and pastel
13½ × 18½ in (32.2 × 47 cm)
Signed and dated 1951
Commissioned as the Evelyn Award, 1951
(R2474)

The City walls, 'the finest belt of stonework which could be found in the country', have since 1889, when the last section, between Bootham Bar and Monk Bar, was opened to the public, provided a continuous secluded footpath round the medieval City with many spectacular views of its buildings. After leaving Micklegate Bar and rounding the corner at Tofts Tower one is confronted by a long vista stretching from the North Eastern Railway war memorial, over Lendal Bridge to the Minster, dwarfing the tower of St Wilfrid's Catholic Church, which since 1864 has shared the skyline with it. To appease the conservationists, who were opposed to any interference with the walls and its ramparts, Sir Edwin Lutyens erected, in 1922, a full-size wooden mock-up of his design for the Railway war memorial. After an enquiry the wing walls were reduced in size but the central obelisk was left at its original height of 54 ft.

Reverse of No. 21

22

Unidentified Artist

The Railway Station, date uncertain

Etching on steel
$2\frac{1}{2} \times 4$ in (6.3×10 cm)
Purchased as part of the Evelyn Collection, 1931 (R1765)

23

Unidentified Artist

The Railway Station, published 1861

Etching on steel
$2\frac{3}{8} \times 3\frac{3}{4}$ in (6×9.5 cm)
Published by Rock and Co., London, 20 June 1861
Purchased as part of the Evelyn Collection, 1931 (R1764)

The first train from York, ran on 29 May 1839, from a temporary wooden platform outside the walls in Queen Street but George Hudson wanted a more imposing site for his permanent station. He was able to persuade the various occupants of Friary Gardens to move elsewhere and the Corporation to allow him to breach the walls to gain access. George Townsend Andrews designed the new arches in the walls, the departure building on the west side and the arrival building on the east side, completed by 1841. Linking the station buildings at first was a three-ridged cast-iron and glass train shed but in 1853 it was joined, at its north end, by the Station Hotel (Royal after a visit by Queen Victoria in 1854), also designed by Andrews. The opening of the Scarborough line in 1845 necessitated the building of an extra covered platform next to the walls, while the facilities on the site were completed by a goods warehouse near the easternmost arch through the walls.

24

George Nicholson

North Street Postern, 1825

Pencil
9 × 13 in (22.5 × 32.9 cm)
Dated 18 May 1825
Purchased as part of the Evelyn Collection, 1931 (R1413)

Barker Tower, first referred to as 'the tower on the water of the Ouse behind the tannery', takes its name from the oak bark used by the tanners in the curing of leather. Between here and Lendal Tower on the opposite bank chains were once stretched as part of the City's defences and also to prevent boats slipping through York at night in an attempt to avoid the payment of tolls. The chains were sold in 1553 and thereafter Barker Tower was usually let to the ferryman (and at least one ferrywoman) who carried pedestrians across the river to Lendal Tower 'in summer and winter, fair weather and foul, Sundays and weekdays' from medieval times until the opening of Lendal Bridge in 1863. Now redundant like the ferryman, the tower found a new use in 1879 as a mortuary.

25

George Nicholson

Exterior of North Street Postern, 1825

Pencil
8¾ × 12¾ in (22.5 × 32.6 cm)
Dated 18 May 1825
Purchased as part of the Evelyn Collection, 1931 (R1409)

Next to Barker Tower a narrow gateway, 4 ft wide and 9 ft high, provided a side entrance into the City for travellers on foot or on horse-back. But, narrow as it was, North Street Postern had been enlarged to this size in 1577 by William Foster, mason to the Earl of Huntingdon, Lord President of the Council of the North, so that 'my Lord President['s] great horse may passe through the same', presumably removing the necessity for the Earl to dismount. This privilege cost him 28*s*. 6*d*. The Great North of England Railway, however, had to expend £880 in 1840 when it reconstructed the postern with a wide central arch and two side arches to allow carts to reach their goods depot outside the walls. Of this, £500 went to the Corporation for the right (and was used to restore Walmgate Bar) and £380 to John Buckley for the building work.

The Museum Gardens Area

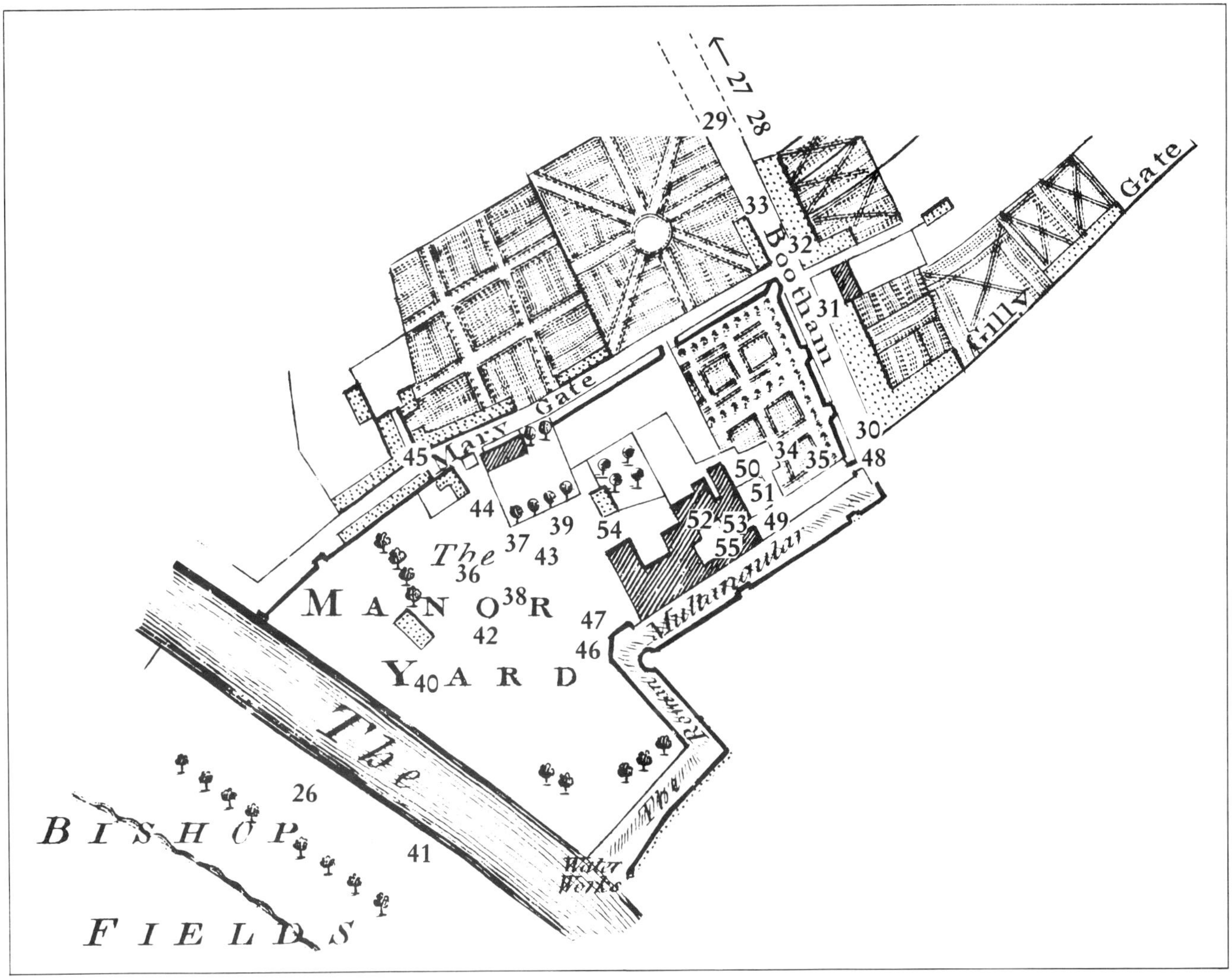

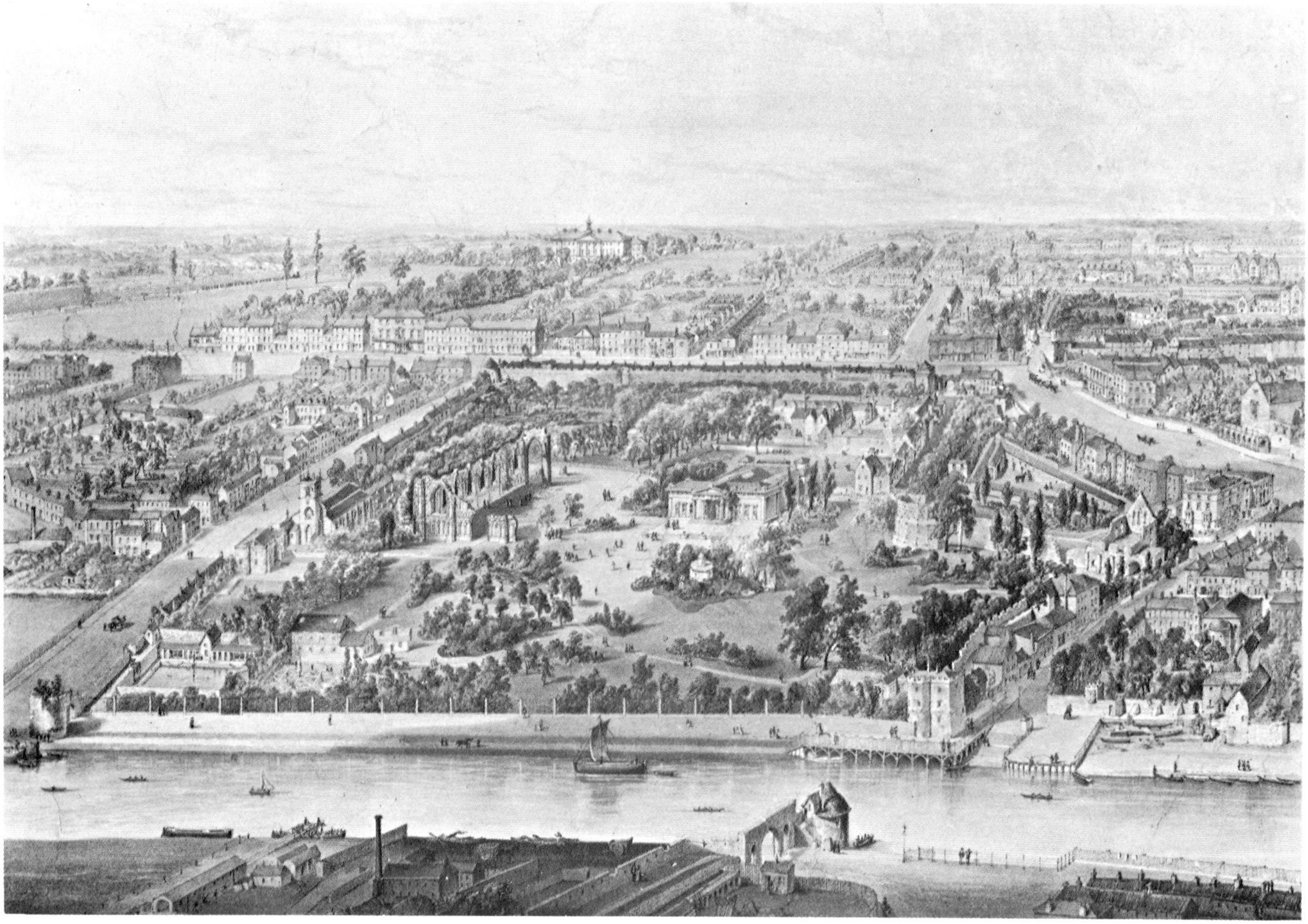

26

John Storey

The Gardens of the Yorkshire Philosophical Society, c. 1860

Colour lithograph
$14\frac{5}{8} \times 21\frac{1}{2}$ in (37.2 × 54.5 cm), image
Printed by William Monkhouse, York
Purchased as part of the Evelyn Collection, 1931 (R1552)

The Yorkshire Philosophical Society, founded in 1822, opened its new museum in 1830, on a three-acre site, once part of the grounds of St Mary's Abbey and including the ruins of the abbey itself. In 1833 an observatory was built on the southern boundary of the site and the following year the remainder of the Manor Shore, another five acres including the abbey gatehouse, was purchased. When the society took possession of this additional area it was 'nothing but a widely extended heap of rubbish and fragments of stone' and it was a condition of the lease that it should be used as a botanic garden. Very soon it was laid out 'without producing that formality which usually accompanies scientific arrangement', although an Elizabethan knot garden with a fountain at its centre was created between the fourteenth-century Hospitium and the river boundary. York's first swimming bath was built in a corner of the grounds in 1837 and opened for a summer season every year until its final closure in 1922.

27

William Moore

'At Clifton', 1846

Pencil and bodycolour
$6\frac{5}{8} \times 10\frac{1}{4}$ in (16.8 × 26.1 cm)
Signed and dated 1846
Provenance unknown (R3119)

Until 1884 the township of Clifton was outside the York boundary, albeit lying in the City parishes of St Olave and St Michael-le-Belfrey. Its affairs were managed by a churchwarden from each of the churches, a constable, a surveyor of the highways and overseers of the poor but, after 1819, by a select committee of villagers. One of these was George Ellison, whose family had farmed in Clifton since, at least, 1649. Their farmhouse, a timber-framed building (shown here on the right), stood in the then main street of Clifton, now Water End. George, the last farming Ellison, died in 1848. When the house was offered for sale in 1898 it was occupied by Curtis Styan. At some time shortly afterwards it was pulled down by Arthur Spottiswoode Jones as part of the continuing conversion of Clifton from 'a charmingly rural spot' into a suburb of York.

28

Attributed to
William Monkhouse

Bootham Asylum, *c.* 1840

Lithograph
8 × 12½ in (20.2 × 31.6 cm), image
Purchased as part of the Evelyn Collection,
1931 (R2890)

Bootham Park Hospital opened on 20 September 1777, built to the designs of John Carr. It was the fifth purpose-built asylum in the country and is now the oldest still being used for its original function. It was once considered a diverting pastime to visit asylums to watch the antics of the inmates. A young lady visiting York in 1812, to her credit, declined the opportunity, 'not thinking it possible to derive any gratification from the melancholy sight of our fellow creatures in a state of insanity'. Had she done so no doubt she would have been very shocked with the conditions inside. At that time the hospital was in the midst of a scandal about the brutal treatment of the patients, the insanitary conditions and misappropriation of its funds. A magistrate, visiting in 1814 found 'that the house is yet in a shocking state'. He discovered 'a number of secret cells in a state of filth horrible beyond description' and described the floor as being covered 'with straw perfectly soaked with urine and excrement'.

29

Henry Cave

Entrance to Sir Arthur Ingram's Hospital, Bootham, 1813

Etching
7¾ × 5¾ in (19.7 × 14.6 cm), image
Signed
Probably purchased as part of the Evelyn Collection, 1931 (R2265)

Before he died in 1640 Sir Arthur Ingram founded a hospital in Bootham for ten poor widows. He acquired the land in 1630 for fifty pounds and the row of two-storeyed brick-built cottages was completed in 1632. To cater for the widows' spiritual needs a chapel, with a low bell tower, was provided in the centre. It was entered through a doorway framed with a richly ornamented late-Norman arch taken from Holy Trinity, Micklegate, having been purchased in October 1630 for 13*s*. 4*d*. Each pensioner had a brick-floored living room with an unheated bedroom above, reached by a wooden staircase. The endowment provided 'for every one of them five pound a piece yearly and a gown every three years and twenty nobles yearly to some honest and able man for reading prayers in the house'. In 1957 J. B. Morrell, having acquired the hospital in exchange for a field behind his house in Burton Stone Lane where new almshouses were built, had the old building converted into four flats.

30

Unidentified Artist

'A View of Bootham Bar', published 1805

Etching and engraving
4⅜ × 7¼ in (11 × 18.4 cm), image
Published by Prince and Cattles, York, 15 January 1805
Probably purchased as part of the Evelyn Collection, 1931 (R2413)

Before July 1831 travellers coming to York from the north had to enter the City through the bottleneck of the barbican and arch of Bootham Bar, which restricted flow of traffic to such an extent that carts and coaches had to queue to negotiate the narrow passage in single file. The residents of Clifton sent a petition to the Corporation asking for the removal of the barbican, deemed to be a great nuisance and 'not fit for any female of respectibility to pass through' because of the droppings of animals on the way to cattle market and its use as a urinal by passers-by. The Bird in Hand Inn, next to the bar, was pulled down when the barbican was removed in 1831 and reopened in a new building on the corner of St Leonard's Place (constructed in 1834) and Bootham, next to the ironmongery of Francis Ward. He traded there from 1801 to 1836, when he handed over to his son, James. On the other side of the road the narrow entrance into Gillygate, further restricted by pillars, was widened in 1909 to admit tram-cars and prevent the destruction of Queen Margaret's Arch.

31

Thomas Shotter Boys

Bootham, *c.* 1840

Pencil, sepia wash and sepia ink
8⅞ × 12 in (22.6 × 30.4 cm)
Provenance unknown (R10)

The great high road from the north entered York along Bootham, a street which, after passing Marygate, presented a complete contrast in the appearance of its two sides. On the south there were 'mean looking houses extending from the round tower at the end of Marygate nearly as far as Bootham Bar and almost wholly concealing from our view the embattled stone wall . . . of St Mary's Abbey'. These were entirely occupied by tradesmen — a saddler, a straw-bonnet maker, a baker, two butchers, a dealer in earthenware, a painter, a hairdresser, a shoemaker, a whitesmith, a publican, a seedsman and an ironmonger. On the other side a few shopkeepers were interspersed among the larger houses, of gentry and professional people. In an observatory behind the house on the left of the Black Horse Inn, Edward Pigott, working with his deaf and dumb collaborator, John Goodricke, discovered, on 21 May 1783, the comet which bears his name.

32

Henry Barlow Carter

Bootham, 1840

Pencil and watercolour with scratching-out
9¼ × 12¾ in (23.5 × 32.4 cm)
Signed
Purchased as part of the Evelyn Collection, 1931 (R44)

Marygate Tower, used from 1540 to store the records of the Yorkshire monasteries, was extensively damaged by a mine during the Civil War. In carrying out repairs the stonemasons rather clumsily joined their rebuilt wall on to the undamaged portion. For many years the evidence of their slipshod work was hidden by a house built against the tower but when this was removed in 1896 there, for all to see, was the exposed rubble infill between the old and new walls of dressed stone. The booths are a reminder of the derivation — *at the booths* — of the name of this street. Drake, in 1735, said that they were erected at the weekly market of the abbots of St Mary's, in whose jurisdiction the south side of Bootham lay. The first mention of the name is in *c.* 1145 and, while there is no evidence of the fair until 1318, it is probable that farmers, before then, brought their produce to sell here, free from the tolls to which they would have been subject within the City.

33

Edwin Ridsdale Tate

The Abbey Walls from Bootham, 1915

Pen and black ink with two sepia photographs
$14^{1}/_{8} \times 36^{1}/_{4}$ in (36×92.1 cm)
Signed and dated 1915
Purchased as part of the Evelyn Collection, 1931 (R3087)

The abbey precinct walls still remain on the Bootham and Marygate sides. The wall between the gatehouse and the water tower was started in 1318, a continuation of the sections along Bootham and between Marygate Tower and the gatehouse, begun in 1266. In 1877 these walls, obscured by houses both in Bootham and Marygate, became the property of the Yorkshire Philosophical Society. The houses at the lower end of Marygate were removed by 1895 and the wall behind them was reinstated. The Society, which thought that Bootham would also be more attractive if the wall there were cleared, then started a campaign to persuade the owners of the houses to remove them. In 1896, during the rebuilding of the White Horse Hotel, half the round tower at its north end was exposed and at the same time, the house next to Marygate Tower was pulled down. To do this the Society had had to borrow money from the Corporation to buy the house and, consequently, made over to it all the walls except the gatehouse. Three cottages between the two cleared sites were later bought jointly by the Corporation and the Society. After they were demolished in 1914, Ridsdale Tate made this drawing showing how the walls had appeared before they were built against and included two photographs to show the progress already made in clearing them. Finally, after the Second World War, two shops were pulled down at the City end of this site, which is now a rest garden. The clearances in Marygate had been completed in 1921 with the removal of a number of tall, narrow, insanitary houses at the top of the street.

34

Henry Rushbury

Bootham Bar, 1965

Pencil, watercolour and black crayon with scratching-out
14¼ × 17¾ in (36.2 × 45.1 cm), image
Signed and dated 1965
Purchased with the aid of a grant from the Museums and Galleries Commission through the Victoria and Albert Museum, 1988 (R3059)

George Walker Milburn died in 1941, aged ninety-seven and said to be the oldest sculptor in the country. His business then passed to his son, Wilfrid, who kept it going until his death in 1949. Since then their stone-yard (behind the short stretch of wall to the right of the bar) has been occupied by a ladies' lavatory. In 1889 a flight of stone steps was constructed, leading from outside the walls to the walkway within to open the last section of the walls to the public. The opening of the walk from Monk Bar to Bootham Bar had, at first, been fiercely opposed by Dean Purey-Cust and Edwin Gray, whose privacy was preserved by the walls which bounded their gardens. The Dean was advised 'to practise that charity and generosity which he preached in those beautiful sermons he composed especially for working men'. Both he and Gray eventually retreated from their entrenched positions and the completely restored walls were opened by the Corporation with full ceremony.

35

Myles Birket Foster

Bootham Bar, 1880s

Pencil, watercolour and bodycolour
4 × 5⅝ in (10.1 × 14.3 cm), image
Signed
Purchased, 1961 (R2479)

Shorn of its barbican, Bootham Bar no longer presented any obstruction to pedestrians and vehicles. St Leonard's Place (to the right) had been constructed in the years 1835–42 while the open space of Exhibition Square opposite the bar was created in 1878–9. The wall next to the bar was used for notices; a permanent one amongst the more ephemeral advertised the *York Herald*, a newspaper which changed from being weekly to daily on 1 January 1874 before becoming the *Yorkshire Herald* in 1890 in celebration of its centenary. Behind the wall, in the 1840s, Ralph Weatherley (not 'W Weathraly' as recorded by the artist), had established a builder's yard. He retired in 1866 and his brother Robert, who carried on the business, moved to Lord Mayor's Walk in *c*. 1888, making way for the sculptor, George Walker Milburn, who was to carve his statue of William Etty there. Ralph Weatherley's last public act had been the supervision of the work of clearing and paving Exhibition Square.

36

Thomas Rowlandson

St Mary's Abbey Gateway,
***c.* 1800**

Pencil, watercolour and pen and ink
4⅞ × 14⅞ in (12.3 × 37.8 cm)
Purchased with the aid of a grant from the Victoria and Albert Museum, 1985 (R2692)

This drawing, which appears to have been made on two adjoining pages of a sketchbook, was probably executed on the spot. It presumably provided the basis for the finished drawing No. 37.

37

Thomas Rowlandson

St Mary's Abbey Gateway, (?)1801

Pencil, watercolour and pen and ink
$8\frac{1}{8} \times 13\frac{5}{8}$ in (20.6 × 34.7 cm)
Signed and dated 1801
Purchased (as 'Old Gateway to Manor Shore') as part of the Evelyn Collection, 1931 (R1718)

The remains of the late twelfth-century abbey gatehouse stand on the line of a Roman road. In the early eighteenth century it was almost complete. By the time this drawing was made one hundred years later, however, it had lost all but the arch at the Marygate end and the flanking walls of the entrance passage-way, against which extensions had been built in *c*. 1470 to provide suites of rooms for important guests to the abbey. The building on the north-east, linking the gatehouse to St Olave's Church, was also an eighteenth-century casualty but the other, St Mary's Lodge, survives. In 1840, soon after it was acquired by the Yorkshire Philosophical Society, it was modernized to become the home of the first keeper of the Society's museum, John Phillips. It was given a new interior and the hipped, tiled roof was replaced by a lower pitched roof within a stone parapet.

38

William Richardson

St Mary's Abbey, *c.* 1843

Pencil, watercolour and bodycolour
$12\frac{1}{2} \times 19\frac{7}{8}$ in (31.8×50.5 cm)
Presented by the family of the late J. B. Morrell, Esq., 1964 (R3023)

39

William Richardson

St Mary's Abbey, 1843

Pencil, watercolour and bodycolour
$9\frac{7}{8} \times 12\frac{3}{4}$ in (25.2×32.5 cm)
Signed and dated 1843
Presented by the family of the late J. B. Morrell, Esq., 1964 (R1793)

40

William Lodge

St Mary's Abbey, *c.* 1680

Pencil, pen and ink, and grey wash
$5\frac{5}{8} \times 9\frac{3}{4}$ in (14.3×24.9 cm)
Purchased as part of the Evelyn Collection, 1931 (R1854)

The origins of St Mary's Abbey, the wealthiest and most powerful monastery in the north of England, are to be found at Whitby in the 1070s. There Reinfrid, a knight who served under William the Conqueror and subsequently became a monk at Evesham, founded a monastic community. This community split after a few years, whereupon a number of monks moved to Lastingham. Alan Rufus, son of Eudo, Earl of Brittany, offered these monks the church of St Olave in Marygate with four acres of land and by 1086 their presence in York is recorded in the Domesday Book. Two years later William Rufus gave the community a larger piece of land next to the church where they could build an abbey. The King himself laid the foundation stone, in 1089, of a Romanesque church dedicated to St Mary and built, because of the shape of the site, on a north-east alignment. It was destroyed on 4 June 1137 by a disastrous fire which swept through York, burning down the Minster and thirty-nine parish churches as well. Although it was extensively remodelled after the fire, it was later decided to build another, larger, church enveloping the Romanesque building. The first stone of this Gothic church, now ruined, was laid on 24 April 1270.

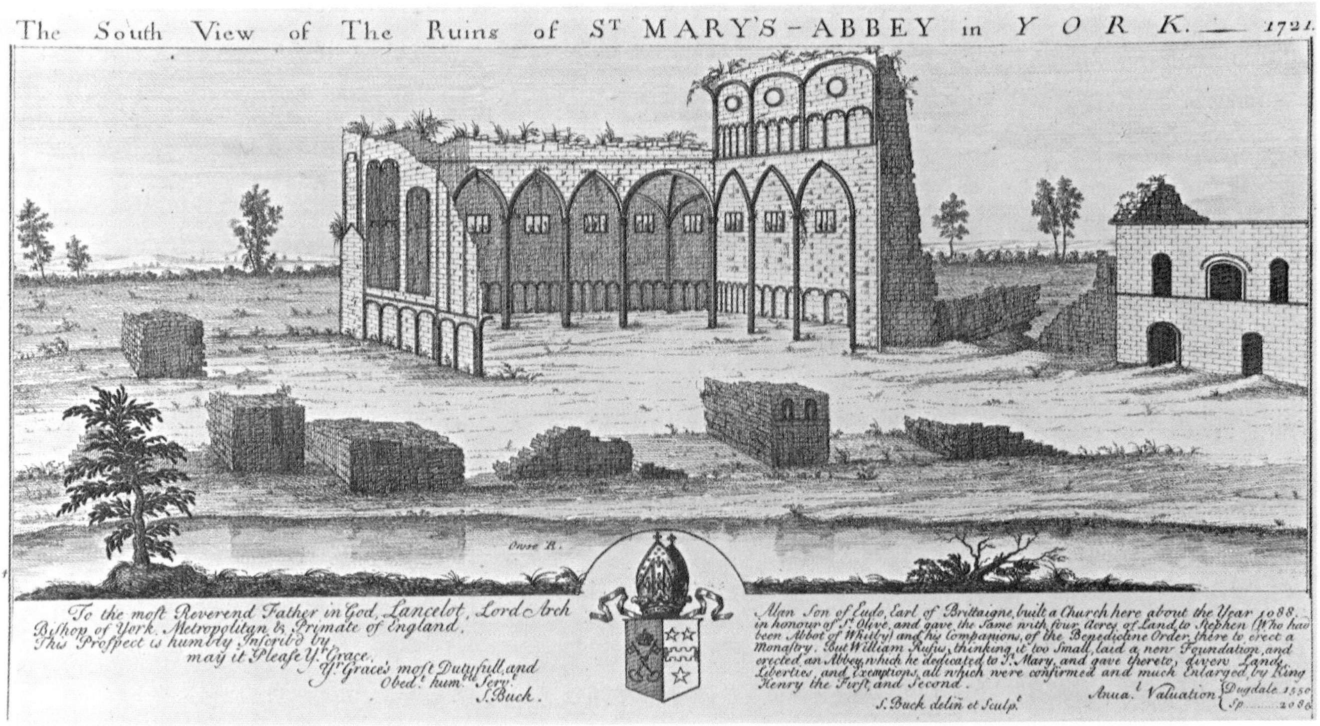

41

Samuel Buck

'The South View of The Ruins of St Mary's – Abbey in York', 1721

Etching
7⅜ × 14⅜ in (18.7 × 36.5 cm)
Purchased as part of the Evelyn Collection, 1931 (R2492)

The second abbey church of St Mary's, which took twenty-four years to build, was completed, unlike most medieval churches, to its original design. It was to have only one major addition, a tower built to replace the steeple which had been struck by lightning in 1377. Of the other buildings which occupied the abbey site, the cloister and warming house were built at the end of the thirteenth century, the original chapter house was made into a vestibule for a new chapter house at the same time and the dormitory was rebuilt early in the fourteenth century.

All the major landowners of Yorkshire had been benefactors of the abbey, which acquired great wealth and attracted many recruits. However, in 1132 the prior and thirteen monks, dissatisfied with the way the monastic life had altered from the traditional Benedictine rule, left to found a new Cistercian house at Fountains. But despite this seccession, the abbey continued to flourish and, at the same time, benefit the City by providing employment for both craftsmen and unskilled men, as well as feeding the poor and supporting the sick.

42

George Cuitt

St Mary's, 1834

Etching
$13\frac{3}{4} \times 10\frac{3}{8}$ in (35×26.5 cm), image
Signed and dated 1834
Probably purchased as part of the Evelyn Collection, 1931 (R3030)

By the sixteenth century, the popularity of the religious orders was at a low ebb and little opposition was raised against Henry VIII's Dissolution of the Monasteries, which, it was said, was initiated to check the widespread corruption to be found amongst their occupants. His break with Rome and assumption of the role of head of the church gave him the right to involve himself in such matters but the real reason was his pressing need for more money. St Mary's Abbey was the richest house in the North with an annual income of £2,091 4*s*. 7¼*d*. It escaped the first round of closures, which was limited to houses valued at less than £200 a year, but following the success of this venture Henry next turned to the richer establishments and so the fifty monks, including the abbot, prior, sub-prior and one novice, of St Mary's surrendered their abbey to the King on 26 November 1539.

43

John White Abbott

'A Ruin at York called King's Palace' (actually St Mary's Abbey), 1791

Pencil, watercolour and pen and ink, on the artist's original wash-line mount
7½ × 9½ in (19 × 24.2 cm)
Signed and dated 13 June 1791 (on the reverse)
Purchased, 1947 (R3)

Some small demolition of the abbey buildings started shortly after the Dissolution but it was not until 1568–70 that any major loss of its fabric occurred. The choir, transepts and chapter house were taken down so that improvements could be made to the abbot's house which had become the headquarters of the Council in the North. The nave escaped this fate as, with its clerestory lowered and its body made into an open courtyard, its aisles were turned into out-buildings serving the other surviving buildings round the cloister. In later years more and more buildings were demolished and their stones reused — for repairs to Ouse Bridge, the construction of the County Gaol in 1701, the rebuilding of St Olave's church in 1705 and, farther afield, for repairs to Beverley Minster in 1717. By the beginning of the nineteenth century all that was left of any substance, above ground, of the once magnificent abbey comprised the lower courses of the west end, the wall of the north aisle of the nave and the north-east pier of the crossing of the church. Its grounds became meadows whose harvest was sometimes stacked in ricks in the remaining nave aisle (as shown here).

44

George Nicholson

St Mary's Abbey, 1827

Etching
4⅞ × 7⅛ in (12.3 × 18.1 cm), image
Signed and dated 1827
Probably purchased as part of the Evelyn
Collection, 1931 (R3148)

45

George Nicholson

Gateway to St Mary's Abbey, 1827

Etching
4⅞ × 7⅛ in (12.3 × 18 cm), image
Signed and dated 1827
Provenance unknown (R2614)

Before the Dissolution of the Monsasteries in the sixteenth century a porter lived in the gatehouse and the lower portion of St Mary's Lodge was the abbey prison. Here malefactors in the liberty of St Mary's were confined after their cases had been heard in the courthouse above. More serious crimes were dealt with at the abbot's gallows, near Lady Mill in Burton Stone Lane. By the beginning of the nineteenth century the lodge had become a public house, the Bay Horse; this was a favourite name in Yorkshire and one borne by ten taverns in the City at that time. After the conversion of the lodge into a house in 1840 the Bay Horse transferred to a building against the abbey walls further down Marygate. This was condemned by the Corporation as insanitary in 1894 and a new (and the present) Bay Horse took its place on the other side of the road as part of an estate of terraced houses then being built between Marygate and the railway.

46

Moses Griffith

Multangular Tower, 1777

Pencil, watercolour and pen and ink
$5\frac{3}{4} \times 7\frac{1}{2}$ in (14.6×18.9 cm), image
Signed
Purchased, 1913 (R372)

The Precinct of St Mary's Abbey was surrounded by its own walls. On the south-east they ran parallel to the City's defences with a ditch in the no man's land in between, the cause of much strife between the abbey and the City. These walls were removed by the eighteenth century leaving, as the boundary on that side of the Manor Shore, part of the late thirteenth-century City walls, which had been built on top of the fourth-century walls of the Roman fortress. Its west angle tower, once known as Elrondyng but now much more prosaically as the Multangular Tower in reference to its nine faces, stands to some nineteen feet, with a string course of red tiles at eight feet. The medieval builders increased the height of the tower by eleven feet and pierced each of the faces with a cruciform arrow-slit. The Roman wall continues towards Lendal, although some of the height has since been lost, perhaps in the demolition of the buildings against its inner face, during the clearance of Mint Yard in the nineteenth century.

47

William Moore

Multangular Tower, 1846

Pencil and bodycolour
$6\frac{5}{8} \times 10\frac{1}{4}$ in (16.8×25.9 cm)
Signed and dated 1846
Purchased as part of the Evelyn Collection, 1931 (R3116)

In 'the formation of an English Botanical Garden' the Yorkshire Philosophical Society installed two fountains. One was in the herb garden in front of the Hospitium and the other was placed in a circular pool near the Multangular Tower. The latter fountain was the gift, in 1838, of J. Bradwell, an iron founder of Micklegate. In 1917, after the pool was filled in, the fountain disappeared. It was found fifty years later, in 1967, in the undergrowth of a garden in Manor Drive, Acomb, without its stem and upper basin. Restored and repainted, it was used as a garden ornament until 1987, when it was acquired by the York Civic Trust and mounted on a stone plinth at Fairfax House. There the surviving pieces make 'a fine receptacle for flowers to brighten the courtyard'.

48

Francis Bedford

'Ancient Gateway to the Yorkshire School for the Blind', *c.* 1840–43

Two-toned lithograph
9⅝ × 7 in (24.4 × 17.8 cm), image
Printed by William Monkhouse, York
Purchased as part of the Evelyn Collection, 1931 (R2889)

When the Exhibition Building (now the Art Gallery) was being built for the second Yorkshire Fine Art and Industrial Exhibition of 1879 a new square (Exhibition Square) was created between it and St Leonard's Place. This necessitated the demolition, in 1878, of a group of buildings on one side of Queen Margaret's Arch, including the Bird in Hand Inn and the shop of Mrs Mary Bussey Ward, who had taken over the ironmongery business on the death of her husband, James, in 1838. The postern tower, the premises of Edward Bearpark, nurseryman and seedsman, and the arch had been built in 1497 for an intended visit to York of Henry VII, who was to stay with the abbot of St Mary's. This gateway was for 'his pleasure and passage to the mynster' and not, as the name by which it is known would imply, for the convenience of his daughter, Margaret Tudor, who passed through York in 1503, on her way to marry James IV of Scotland. The principal beneficiary, however, was the abbot, who could now reach the City more easily than by using the main abbey entrance in Marygate. Two attempts to pull it down, in 1908 and 1969, to improve traffic flows have been successfully resisted.

49

John Brown(e)

Entrance to the King's Manor, 1817

Pencil and bodycolour
$17\frac{1}{4} \times 13\frac{1}{2}$ in (34.8 × 34.5 cm), image
Signed and dated 1817
Purchased as part of the Evelyn Collection, 1931 (R1571)

The south doorway on the east front of the King's Manor was given a highly ornamental stone surround ensigned with the crowned initials IR for James I. It was probably inserted early in his reign (1603–1625) as he had, on his first visit to York, ordered that the Manor be repaired and converted to a royal palace for use on his journeys between London and Scotland. The royal arms over the door, the full heraldic achievement of the Stuart monarchs, were added during the reign of Charles I (1625–1649). Carved in stone, they deteriorated to such an extent that by 1972 they were almost indecipherable. The arms were then recarved and painted and the newly restored achievement was unveiled on 21 October by Mrs Jean Coggan accompanied by her husband, the Archbishop of York, and a company of the Sealed Knot.

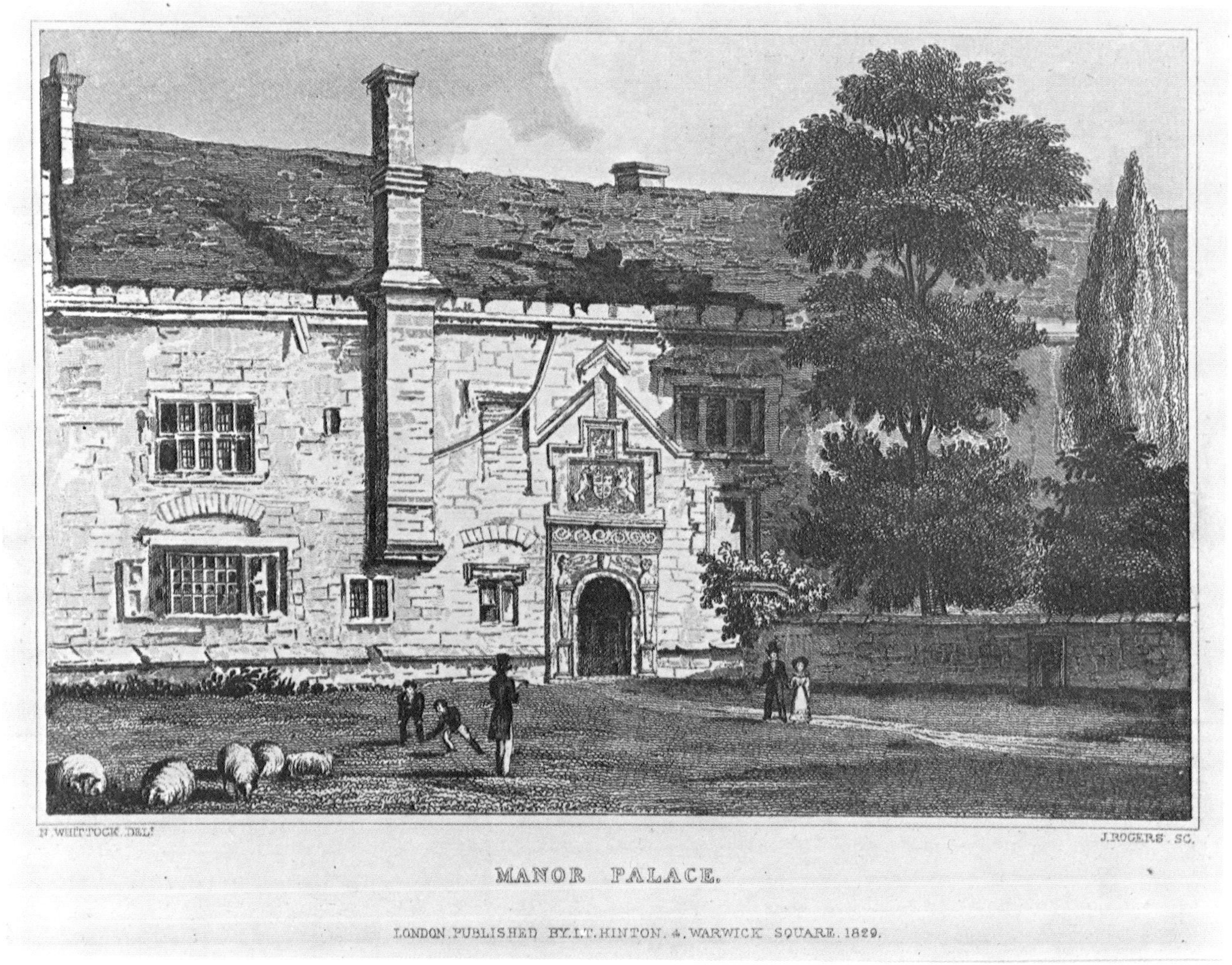

50

J. Rogers
after Nathaniel Whittock

'Manor Palace', 1829

Etching on steel
$3\frac{7}{8} \times 5\frac{3}{4}$ in (9.8 × 14.7 cm), image
Published by I. T. Hinton, 4 Warwick Square, London, 1829
Acquired by 1934 (R3149)

The blocked-up windows and a relieving arch too small for the window below testify to the many vicissitudes undergone by the east range of the King's Manor since it was built in *c.* 1480. The relieving arches mark the position of two of the original terracotta windows which with others were replaced during the sixteenth century. The chimney-stack was added in the seventeenth century, perhaps at the same time as an opening was made for a new doorway with an ornamental stone surround. Behind the wall is the part of the Manor occupied at this time by a 'Boarding School for Ladies'.

51

William Monkhouse

The Yorkshire School for the Blind, *c.* 1840

Lithograph
6⅝ × 9⅜ in (16.7 × 23.8 cm), image
Purchased as part of the Evelyn Collection, 1931 (R3150)

In 1835 the Yorkshire School for the Blind, founded by William Wilberforce in 1833, acquired the lease of the whole of the King's Manor round its front quadrangle, remaining there until 1956. It was probably with the arrival of the handicapped pupils that all the ground-floor and some of the upper-floor windows were replaced. The wall has been moved to satisfy one of the shibboleths of the Victorians, the segregation of the sexes: the boys entered their part of the school through the less elaborate doorway while the girls' entrance to their classrooms was in the sixteenth-century extension hidden in this view by trees. Visitors to the school entered by the main doorway where they were confronted by a notice advising them that 'Subscribers, customers and their friends are admitted free. Any strangers desirous of inspecting the school rooms and workshops will be supplied with a ticket for that purpose'. These could be bought in the workroom but on Thursdays the purchase of a ticket for the weekly concert served the same purpose.

52

John Harper

Doorway in the King's Manor, 1840

Pencil
$7\frac{1}{4} \times 6\frac{1}{2}$ in (18.4 × 16.4 cm), image
Probably presented by A. Laws, Esq., 1935
(R1649)

The front quadrangle of the King's Manor was created by extensions to each leg of the U-shaped medieval building, which were then joined by a single-storied gallery between them, built during the Presidency of Lord Sheffield from 1603 to 1619. When Thomas Wentworth, Earl of Strafford, President from 1628 to 1641, added an upper floor to this gallery he had the 'unbecoming arrogance in putting up his own arms in one of the king's palaces' over the central doorway as shown here. It is often stated, quite erroneously, that this was the subject of one of the articles of impeachment against him. He was charged, in November 1640, with illegal and tyrannical rule in Ireland but the impeachment failed and a Bill of Attainder was brought against him instead, which lead to his being beheaded on 12 May 1641.

53

John Harper

Entrance to the King's Manor, 1840

Pencil and bodycolour
$8\frac{1}{2} \times 6\frac{5}{8}$ in (21.5 × 16.9 cm), image
Probably presented by A. Laws, Esq., 1935
(R1658)

This second, north, doorway on the east front of the King's Manor is an original opening of *c*. 1480. However, its surround, of a similar style and date to that of a companion door further to the south (see No. 49), was removed here *c*. 1830 from the west elevation of the main court (where it is recorded in No. 55).

54

Frederick Nash

'View of the Ruins adjoining the South Transept of the Church, with the Palace of K. James 2nd and the Tower of the Minster in the Background', 1829

Lithograph
11⅜ × 17½ in (28.8 × 44.6 cm), image
Printed by Charles Hullmandel
Published by the Society of Antiquaries of London, 23 April 1829
Acquired by 1934 (R2506)

The collections of the Yorkshire Philosophical Society soon outgrew its museum in a building next to Ouse Bridge and it became essential to find larger premises. It was proposed to build a new museum on the Manor Shore, a plot of ground 'not very profitably occupied'. At the same time the Society hoped to be able to preserve what remained of the abbey church thus preventing 'the total decay into which the venerable ruin seemed rapidly falling' so that 'this interesting monument of piety taste, and skill of past ages, might not be added to the long list of architectural beauties by which York was once adorned, and of the existence of which no trace is now to be found but in the tablets of artists'. Three acres were transferred to the Society by the Crown on 2 February 1829 but the Archbishop of York had, on 24 October 1827, already laid the foundation stone of the museum which was to be built just to the south-east of the abbey chapter house. To determine the nature of the soil on which the museum was to stand and to explore the site of the principal buildings of the monastery the Society made extensive excavations. These exposed, amongst the remains of other buildings, the piers and walls of the chapter house vestibule leading to the portal of the chapter house itself, marked by two ornamented columns.

55

Henry Cave

King's Manor, *c.* 1822

Pencil, watercolour and bodycolour with scratching-out
11 × 16½ in (28 × 41.8 cm)
Provenance unknown (R45)

The buildings of St Mary's Abbey, surrendered to the Crown in 1539, included the abbot's residence to the north-east of the church. His house had been originally built in *c*. 1270 but was considerably altered in *c*. 1480. After the departure of the abbots it was granted, under its new name of King's Manor, to the Council in the North. The building was altered and added to by various Presidents of the Council from 1560 until the Council's abolition in 1641. During the Commonwealth it became the residence of the Governor of the City of York, and then, after the Restoration, its uses were many and varied. It was the home of a number of schools, parts were in private occupation (one tenant was Francis Place) and the banqueting hall was used as an assembly room. Since 1958 it has belonged to the Corporation who, in 1963, leased it to the University of York, the present occupiers. During the period 1712–1835, when it was occupied by Mr Lumley's Boarding School for Ladies (where Cave was drawing master), the rainwater was carried from the eaves by a number of pipes taking the most direct route to the ground, even, it would appear, with trees growing between them and the building. The elaborate doorway was moved, later in the century, to its present position on the east front (see No. 53).

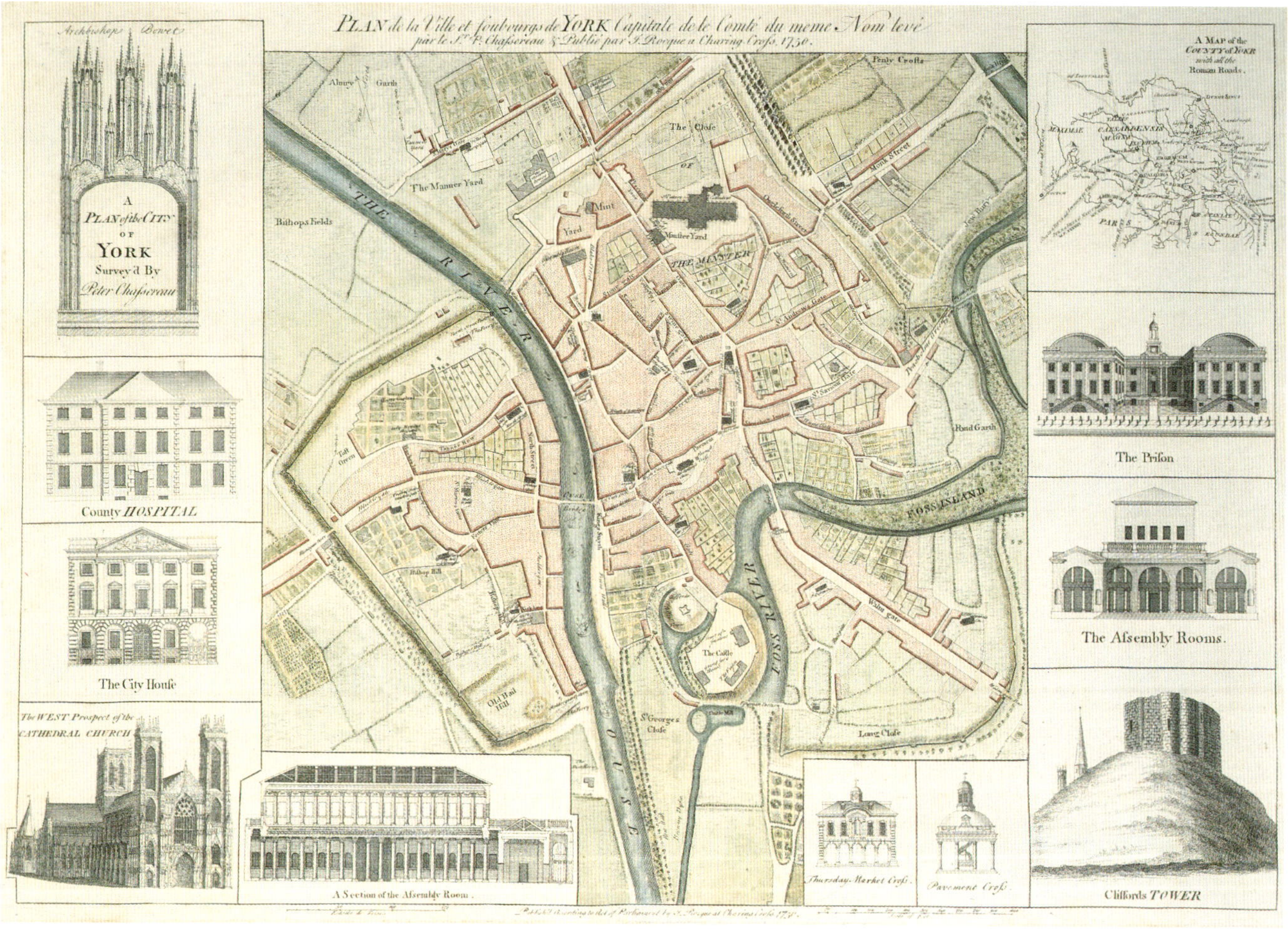

56

John Rocque
after Peter Chassereau

'Plan de la Ville et foubourgs de York Capitale de le Comté du meme Nom' (Plan of the City of York), 1750

Coloured etching
18 × 26¼ in (46 × 66.7 cm)
Published by John Rocque, Charing Cross, 1750
Acquired by 1934 (R2739)

Peter Chassereau's map is one in a succession that has been produced for a variety of purposes, both civil and military, since the earliest known was published in the middle of the sixteenth century. Apparently a new survey, it shows the built-up areas within the walls and alongside the main roads approaching the City by stippled blocks, with indications of building-locked gardens within. Only the principal buildings, ecclesiastic and public, are specifically marked. The absence of the Mansion House on the plan itself may suggest that the survey was made earlier than the 1750 publication date, but it is included in the elevations of buildings in the margins (such marginal illustrations were an innovation of John Cossin in *c.* 1727). Of the buildings depicted the two market crosses have been pulled down, the County Hospital was rebuilt between 1851 and 1860 and the Assembly Rooms were given a new façade in 1828 when Blake Street was widened.

The Central Area

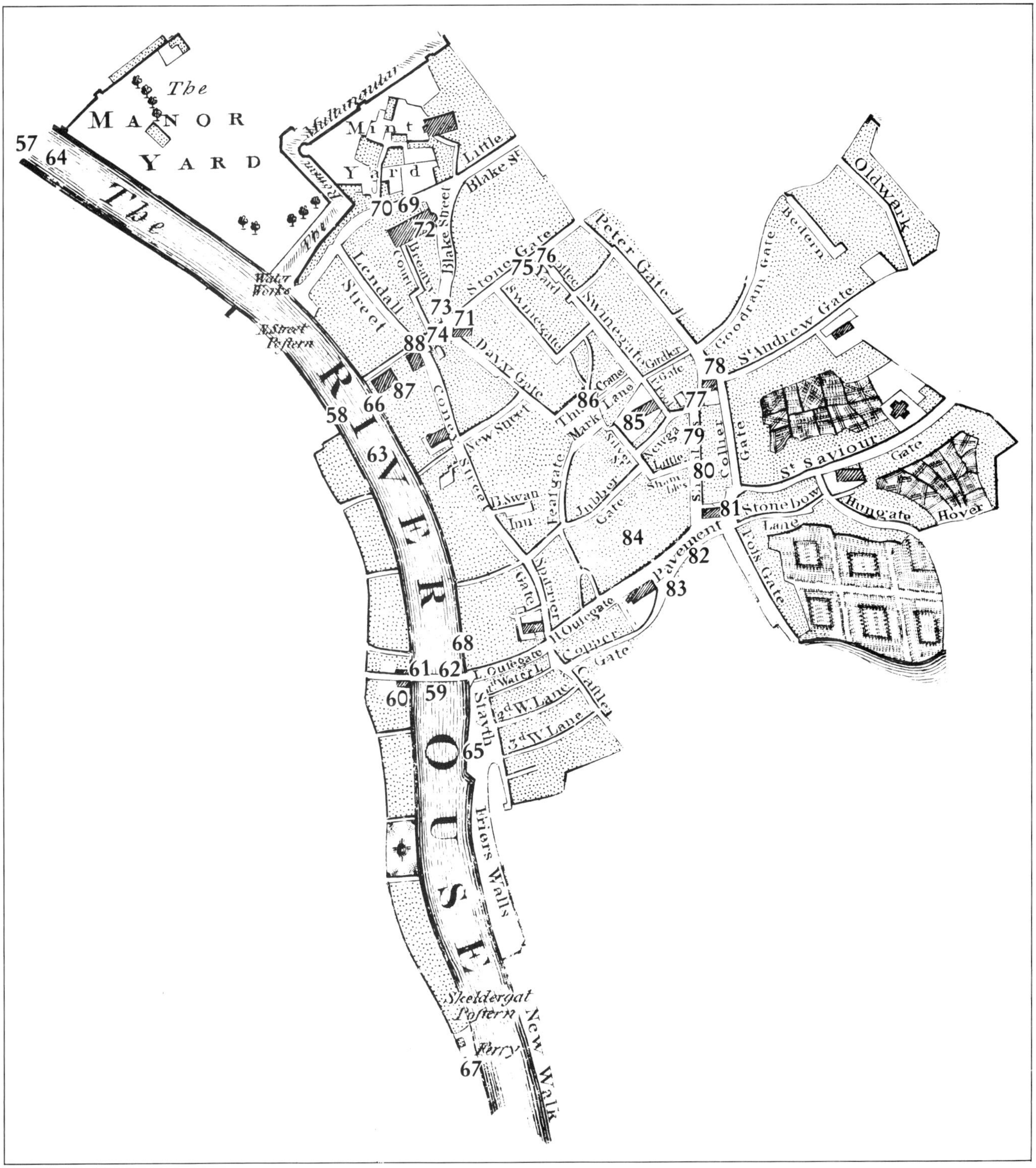

57

Francis Place

York from St Mary's Tower, c. 1705

Pencil, watercolour and pen and ink
$4\frac{3}{4} \times 9\frac{5}{8}$ in (12.1 × 24.5 cm)
Purchased as part of the Evelyn Collection, 1931 (R1858)

The stone walls of the medieval river frontage, well advanced from the natural river banks to provide more land space, a scarce commodity within the confines of the bar walls, are framed by Lendal Tower (left) and Barker Tower (right). Between them chains were once stretched to complete the City's defences. The mud in front of the riverside walls testifies to the tidal state of the river at the time while the ruined wall of St Mary's Abbey (in the foreground) shows that the citizens of York have, since the Dissolution, found other uses for its stones.

58

Henry Cave

On the River Ouse looking upstream, *c.* 1800

Pencil
$9\frac{1}{8} \times 13\frac{1}{4}$ in (23.3×33.8 cm)
Signed and illegibly dated (on the reverse)
Purchased as part of the Evelyn Collection, 1931 (R3167)

The defensive chains mentioned under No. 57 were sold in 1553 and Lendal Tower (centre) had to wait until 1616 before it found a new use — housing the header tank for the City's new water supply. This scheme failed in 1632 but an improved system was installed in 1677. The tower was raised to increase the head of water which was pumped to it, in succession, by a water wheel, a horse gin and a Newcomen steam engine. At the beginning of the nineteenth century this water supply was inadequate for the expanding city and a new (the present) waterworks was opened at Acomb Landing in 1849. After this the tank was removed and the tower, lowered by 10 ft to its original height, was given a crenallated parapet. St Olave's tower (in the distance) appears to be unduly large.

59

Henry Cave

The Old and New Ouse Bridges, 1823

Lithograph
1¾ × 5⅞ in (4.5 × 14.9 cm) (each of two separate images)
Printed by Charles Hullmandel
Published by J. & G. Todd, Stonegate, 1823
Purchased as part of the Evelyn Collection, 1931 (R1763)

Completion of the new Ouse Bridge was delayed by financial problems so it was not until 1 January 1818 that pedestrians were able to cross the first half, 27 ft wide. Then, on 19 August 1820, the whole bridge, 40 ft wide, was opened to all traffic. The five arches of the old bridge were replaced by three — a central arch of 75 ft flanked by two of 64 ft. From 1820 to 1829 tolls were collected from 'a square brick box . . . placed about half way and rather to one side' to help pay for the construction. When they were abolished there was a grand procession through the City to celebrate 'the removal of this oppressive toll'. However beneficial the new bridge proved to be, the old one was remembered with regret. Mary Ann Hughes, wife of the vicar of Uffington, wrote in her diary in 1824 that she had walked over the new bridge which 'I sorely grieved to find replacing the old Rialto-looking one so familiar to me from prints'.

60

Joseph Southall

Ouse Bridge from Queen's Staithe, 1943

Pencil, watercolour and bodycolour
14¾ × 20½ in (37.5 × 52 cm), image
Signed and dated 1943
Purchased from the artist, 1943 (R511)

Low Ousegate was widened in 1820 to improve the approach to the newly-widened bridge and a terrace of new houses and shops was built between the bridge and St Michael, Spurriergate. Behind them the Brett brothers established their City Brewery in 1858, drawing their water, not from the Ouse, but from a very deep artesian well within the brewery to produce ales and stouts of 'the highest possible standard of excellence in purity and fine quality'.

61

Henry Cave

Interior of St William's Chapel during Demolition, *c.* 1810

Pencil
$9\frac{7}{8} \times 13\frac{7}{8}$ in (25.1×35.2 cm)
Signed
Purchased as part of the Evelyn Collection, 1931 (R3049)

The medieval bridge, the single river crossing on the Ouse until the opening of Selby Bridge in 1792, was only 16 ft wide, with a footpath on the south side. With the steep slope of the central arch it formed a considerable hindrance to commerce and so by 1795 the Corporation was considering the possibility of either rebuilding or widening the bridge. Many schemes were proposed and discarded until 1809 when a competition was won by Peter Atkinson the younger with a design using the piers of the old bridge. After an inspection by Thomas Harrison of Chester it was decided that complete rebuilding was necessary and Atkinson submitted a new design. The first stage was to build half of the new bridge on the upstream side of the old. St William's Chapel stood in the way, however, and had to be demolished in time for the foundation stone to be laid on 10 December 1810.

62

Joseph Halfpenny

Entrance to St William's Chapel, 1807

Etching
11¼ × 9 in (28.5 × 23 cm)
Published by Joseph Halfpenny, York, 1 November 1807
Provenance unknown (R2372)

While little remains of St William's Chapel, apart from a few fragments in the Yorkshire Museum, the detailed drawings made by Halfpenny and Cave confirm, on the basis of the architectural style recorded, that it was first built in the late-twelfth century. Parts of the earlier structure were used when it was rebuilt early in the next century. The late-Norman doorway of the chapel shows a profusion of rich, well-preserved ornamentation.

63

William James Boddy

St Martin's from the River Ouse, 1910

Pencil and watercolour
$12\frac{3}{8} \times 10$ in (31.4×25.3 cm)
Signed and dated 1910
Presented by W. Hurworth, Esq., 1941 (R2696)

Although dated 1910 this watercolour portrays the scene some forty years earlier — before the dilapidated Queen Anne vicarage of St Martin, Coney Street, was pulled down to make way for a more modern house with a parish room alongside. Behind the vicarage is St Martin's House, purchased by William Etty in April 1848 and his home until his death in November 1849. In the new vicarage the Rev. Major Rider Bresher established a school for boys. By 1889, having outgrown its original premises, this had moved to Tower Street, before finally settling in Castlegate, where it retained its name St Martin's School.

64

Henry Gastineau

'View on the Ouse near York', 1826

Watercolour and bodycolour with scratching-out
$7\frac{1}{4} \times 10\frac{3}{8}$ in (18.6×26.3 cm)
Signed and dated 1826
Purchased with the aid of a grant from the Victoria and Albert Museum, 1980 (R1553)

In the 120 years that have elapsed since Place made his drawing from the same viewpoint (No. 57) the City waterfront has hardly changed. At Marygate Landing, from 1792 until 1845 the home of a shipbuilding firm founded by Cornelius Hill, Humber keels discharge their coal into horse carts. Their leaning masts give the impression that the river is still tidal but the actual explanation is that their coal has been unloaded first from the sides of the holds nearest the bank. It was the high cost of coal brought to York from the pits in this fashion that was a contributory factory in the City's decline at the end of the eighteenth century.

Plying between the banks is one of the many ferries that saved the citizens the long walk to Ouse Bridge. This was the only bridge in the City until Scarborough Bridge (which included a footbridge) was opened in 1845 to carry the new railway to the coast.

65

Joseph Farington

Old Ouse Bridge, 1783

Pencil, wash and pen and ink
17⅞ × 30 in (45.5 × 76.3 cm)
Signed and dated 1783
Purchased with the aid of grants from the Victoria and Albert Museum and the York Civic Trust, 1953 (R1804)

At the end of the twelfth century a six-arched stone bridge was built over the Ouse to replace the previous wooden one. As with other medieval bridges, houses and shops were built on it, precariously cantilevered over the edge to gain valuable space in a crowded city. It was these buildings that were a principal cause of the disaster which struck in 1565: a great volume of snowmelt water, unable to escape through the small arches, came down on the bridge and the buildings with such force that the central pier gave way and two arches and the houses on them were swept away. A ferry was set up almost immediately, soon to be replaced by a floating wooden bridge. For permanent repair the Corporation sought advice from Sir Martin Bowes in London. He sent to York Thomas Harper 'a very expert and painful [painstaking] man, a man of excellent cunning', who recommended 'as the most expedient, ready, surest and cheapest' method of repair that the two destroyed arches of the stone bridge be replaced by one.

66

Henry Rushbury

The Ouse from the Guildhall, 1942

Pencil, watercolour and black crayon
$15\frac{1}{8} \times 18\frac{5}{8}$ in (38.5 × 47.3 cm)
Signed and dated 1942
Possibly purchased, 1945 (R2724)

Upstream of Ouse Bridge the two banks of the river present a considerable contrast. On the east bank the inner chamber of the medieval Guildhall, between a fifteenth-century building and the new Council chamber built *c.* 1810 to replace the old one in St William's Chapel, faces an industrial scene. Barges, from sea-ports downstream and other parts of Britain, unload their cargoes at the wharfs, warehouses and coal-yards of North Street. Many of these buildings, like the Guildhall itself, were severely damaged or destroyed by bombs dropped on 29 April 1942. The peaceful summer scene with pleasure boats moored at the Guildhall terrace and the undamaged buildings opposite all indicate that this view was made before the air raid, or possibly started before the War and finished and signed later.

67

Attributed to John Varley

Old Ouse Bridge, *c.* 1805

Pencil, watercolour and bodycolour with scratching-out
14¾ × 19⅜ in (37.7 × 49.3 cm)
Purchased (as by David Cox), 1932 (R1703)

By October 1566 the new arch of the rebuilt Ouse Bridge, 81 ft wide and 26 ft 3 in above the normal river level, was complete. It was evidently very large for its time: William Campbell, headmaster of Westminster School, in 1586 described it as 'the largest arch I have ever seen' while John Evelyn, in 1654, thought 'the Middle Arch larger than any I have seene in all England'. Houses and shops were allowed to encroach once more on to the new arch until wiser counsels prevailed in 1745 and the Corporation agreed that they should all be pulled down. It took until 1793, however, for them to be removed and replaced with balustrades.

68

John Varley

Old Ouse Bridge and St William's Chapel, 1803 or 1805

Pencil and watercolour
9¼ × 13¾ in (23.2 × 34.7 cm)
Signed and dated 1803 or 1805
Presented by Alderman J. B. Morrell, 1934 (R249)

A chapel had been built on the northern side of the west end of the bridge in the late twelfth century. It was rededicated in 1228, appropriately to St William, formerly Archbishop William Fitzherbert, whose prayers had saved a vast number of people thrown into the river when the wooden bridge collapsed after he had crossed it to retake the throne in the Minster from which he had been deposed in 1147. In 1227 he was canonized at the request of the Dean of York who wanted a local saint for the City. Adjacent to the chapel was the Council chamber with the kidcote, or civic gaol underneath. Also on the bridge, from 1367, was a new latrine constructed on one of the arches, probably 'the place on Owsbridge callyd the pyssing howes' which Agnes Gretehede, widow, kept clean in 1544 for two shillings a year.

69

Henry Cave

Little Blake Street, *c.* 1800

Pencil
$10 \times 13\frac{7}{8}$ in (25.4×35.3 cm)
Presented by T. S. Rowntree, Esq., 1948
(R2423)

Narrow Lop Lane, the more familiar name given to Little Blake Street, leads to the Minster Close. It was entered through Peter Gate, which was pulled down in 1827. This street was widened between 1860 and 1864 and renamed Duncombe Place in honour of Dean Augustus Duncombe who, shortly after his arrival in the City in 1858, had suggested this 'improvement' and contributed considerably to its realization. York then had a vista 'closed by the grandest front of the grandest cathedral'. One house, on the corner of Little Blake Street, was demolished as part of the widening while the others lasted until 1883 when work on the Probate Office started. This opened three years later, and was followed in 1899 by new buildings for the York Dispensary. On the opposite corner of Blake Street was a famous coaching inn, Etridges's Royal Hotel, 'frequented by some of the principal families in the county', which was replaced in 1859 by offices for the York Poor Law Union.

70

Thomas Shotter Boys

Museum Street and Little Blake Street, *c.* 1840

Pencil, wash and ink with scratching-out
12 × 9 in (30.5 × 22.9 cm)
Acquired by 1934 (R1575)

Apart from the removal of Peter Gate at the end of Little Baker Street and the appearance of a very mature poplar tree the passage of forty years has left the streetscape (as recorded in No. 69) unchanged. It was another twenty-four years before, for the first time, an unobstructed view of the whole west front of the Minster could be had. Two vehicles, a four-wheeler drawn by two horses and a two-wheeler with one horse, with their iron-tyred wheels rattling over the cobbles, are a reminder of an era, with still many years to go, when the horse reigned supreme as the means of motive power on the roads.

71

Henry Brown

Blake Street, 1838

Wood engraving
$3\frac{1}{8} \times 4\frac{1}{8}$ in (7.9 × 10.3 cm), image
Signed
Purchased as part of the Evelyn Collection, 1931 (R2994)

In 1816 the York Savings Bank was established in a room on the corner of New Street, with the Lord Mayor as its president. Such was its success that new, larger premises were required. A site on the Blake Street corner of St Helen's Square, then occupied by a large timber-framed house, was acquired in 1829 and in March the next year a Greek-revival building, designed by Pritchett and Watson, was opened for business. At first it had a doorway in the centre of each of its two street elevations but they were replaced early this century by a single door on the corner. This was followed, in 1924, by an extension along Blake Street. On the side of the Square between St Helen's church and Stonegate Mrs Mary Brunton has established a hosiery shop in premises previously occupied by her late husband, Richard Brunton, a gunsmith.

72

William Lindley

'A Perspective View of the inside of the Grand Assembly Room in Blake Street', 1759

Etching and wash
$18^{3}/_{4} \times 20^{1}/_{8}$ in (47.6 × 51.1 cm)
Published November 1759
Purchased as part of the Evelyn Collection, 1931 (R1482)

In 1823 *The Hermit in York* wrote that 'like all other grand monuments of classical taste in England, the great Assembly-Room is disfigured by the barbarian hand of modern innovation. . . . it has fixed between its noble Corinthian columns, a miserable tier of seats or pews, fit only for the accommodation of the market women of Covent Garden, or a Conventicle for Enthusiasts, and which entirely destroy the effect of the columns below, and of the fine capitals with which they are surmounted'. While he obviously appreciated the building designed by the celebrated Lord Burlington and erected between 1730 and 1735, he was not aware of the reason for the presence of these benches in the body of the hall. In 1751 the seats in the aisles had been moved in front of the columns so that they could be used by ladies whose wide hooped skirts prevented them passing through the narrow gaps between the columns, a complaint which had been voiced by the Duchess of Marlborough.

73

Unidentified Artist

St Helen's Square with the Corner of Stonegate and Davygate, *c.* 1830

Pencil, watercolour and pen and ink
11⅛ × 13¼ in (28.2 × 33.8 cm)
Purchased as part of the Evelyn Collection, 1931 (R3166)

Between the perfumery of William Hands at 30 Blake Street and the shop of Richard Brunton at 1 St Helen's Square is the entrance to Stonegate. In this view Brunton's premises rise to four storeys, one more than the building has today. It is often said that the loss of the top storey was due to bomb damage in 1942 but, in fact, its unsafe condition led to its removal a decade earlier. On the other side of Davygate is an hotel opened in 1770 as the York Tavern, one of York's principal coaching houses with stable accommodation for 150 horses. In 1850 it gained the additional name of Harker's when Christopher Harker became its landlord, a name that it retained until it was pulled down in 1928 as part of a scheme for enlarging St Helen's Square and widening Davygate.

74

Thomas Shotter Boys

St Helen's Square, 1837

Pencil, wash and ink
12 × 8⅞ in (30.7 × 22.7 cm)
Purchased as part of the Evelyn Collection, 1931 (R267)

Before it was enlarged to its present size, St Helen's Square was triangular. It narrowed past Blyth and Moore's Public Library into the last remains of Stonegate, which prior to 1745, when the square was created out of St Helen's churchyard, extended right up to the Mansion House. In 1548, after the Reformation, St Helen's Church was declared redundant and was sold to the Corporation, who started to demolish it. However its parishioners obtained an Act of Parliament in 1553 to rebuild it because it stood in a 'principal place' and its suppression had 'defaced and deformed' the City. Its steeple was removed in 1815 and replaced by a lantern tower which was rebuilt in 1876. The church survived another attempt to pull it down in 1910 when its parish was united with St Martin's, Coney Street.

75

Henry Cave

Stonegate, 1813

Etching
$9\frac{7}{8} \times 7\frac{7}{8}$ in (25×20.3 cm), image
Probably purchased as part of the Evelyn Collection, 1931 (R2226)

This ornamented house next door to the Todds' bookshop was occupied in 1813 by a surgeon and apothecary called Palmer. It was described by Henry Cave (whose brother William lived three doors away at 19 Stonegate) as 'bespread with a barbarous mixture of Grecian architectural ornament and others neither Gothic nor Grecian; while an embroidery of foliage and scroll-work appears to be crammed on every part susceptible of ornament, but without grace, because without simplicity'. The building is now bereft of all this elaborate decoration but it may well have still been there when John Ward Knowles, the glass painter, acquired the bookshop (by then Sunter's) in 1874 as a home for his recently-married wife and a workshop for the trade which was to occupy him for the next fifty-seven years. If so it could have been the inspiration for him to decorate his own plain front using carved woodwork and pargetted plaster with, in the words of John Hutchinson, 'splendid disregard for authenticity'.

76

Henry Cave

Todd's Book and Print Warehouse, Stonegate, 1797

Pencil, watercolour and bodycolour
$11\frac{5}{8} \times 15\frac{1}{2}$ in (29.6×39.3 cm)
Purchased as part of the Evelyn Collection, 1931 (R122)

The present important position of York in the bookselling trade is a continuation of a long tradition. For 191 years books were sold at 'The Sign of the Bible' in Stonegate, first, from 1682 to 1731, by Francis Hildyard and then, until 1757, by his son John who was succeeded by John Hinxman. When Hinxman died in 1762 the business was taken over by one of his assistants, John Todd. He was in partnership with Henry Sotheran until 1774, after which he continued alone until his two sons, John the younger and George, were old enough to join him. John the younger survived his younger brother by three years and, on his death in 1837, was followed by Robert Sunter who carried on until 1873. The Todds dealt in both new and secondhand books, advertising that they gave 'full value . . . for Libraries or Parcels of Books'. With these they would stock the shelves in their large warehouse where they also had 'a small collection of prints'.

77

A. H. Findley

A Corner in Kings Square, *c.* 1900

Pencil and watercolour
11¾ × 9 in (29.8 × 23 cm)
Signed
Purchased as part of the Evelyn Collection, 1931 (R1444)

King's Court led out of King's Square, past Holy Trinity Church, through a dog-leg into the Shambles, on a corner on which stood a two-storeyed fourteenth-century timber-framed building joined on to a three-storeyed one of the late eighteenth-century. This accretion of buildings was occupied from *c.* 1890 for some thirty-six years by George Ackroyd, a dealer in second-hand furniture; on the opposite side of the Shambles, W. A. Ellis, butcher, was a tenant from *c.* 1893 to *c.* 1906.

78

Edward Brown

Holy Trinity, King's Court, or Christ Church (before and after restoration), *c.* 1862

Two-toned lithograph
5½ × 4½ in (13.9 × 10.9 cm) (each of two separate images)
Printed by William Monkhouse, Newbald & Stead, York
Purchased as part of the Evelyn Collection, 1931
(R1771)

Holy Trinity or Christ Church, King's Square, stood on a site supposedly once occupied by the palace of the Scandinavian kings. It is first mentioned in 1268 but the remains of an earlier Norman church were found during rebuilding in 1861. In 1829, to widen Colliergate at the entrance to St Andrewgate where several people had been killed in traffic accidents, it was reduced in size and given its odd trapezoidal shape, one that was retained in 1861 when its dilapidated state forced the parishioners to rebuild it. Its parish was united with St Sampson's in 1886 and worship in the church ceased. It was replaced by a much more prosaic use — as a pen for cattle waiting to be slaughtered by the butchers of the Shambles. Finally in 1937, by now totally redundant, it was pulled down to enlarge King's Square.

79

John Skinner Prout

The Shambles, 1839

Pencil
$13\frac{1}{2} \times 8\frac{7}{8}$ in (34.1×22.5 cm)
Signed and dated 5 October 1839
Bequeathed by Dr P. A. Newton, 1987 (R3015)

For over 900 years the Shambles has had associations with butchers. Its name recorded in the Domesday Book as *in macello*, in the provisions market, but by 1316 as *Flesshamelles*, flesh-benches, testifies to the principal trade carried out in the street. On the benches forming part of the windows of their houses the medieval butchers displayed their meat, protected from the weather, but not from flies and bluebottles, by the overhanging jetties of the upper floors or, perhaps, lifting shutters. The animals were slaughtered and the meat prepared in the rooms behind the shops, all this contributing to the unhygienic conditions which led to Bernard Horner, a butcher, being fined, in 1553, for selling 'corrupt and stinking flesh'. Now only one butcher trades in the Shambles, a far cry from the thirty-one in 1895 or even the seventeen in 1280 who paid their *shamel* toll of seventy shillings a year.

80

William Richardson

St Crux's Tower and Pavement from the Shambles, 1881

Pencil, watercolour and bodycolour
$17\frac{1}{2} \times 12\frac{3}{4}$ in (44.5×32.5 cm)
Signed and dated 1881
Purchased as part of the Evelyn Collection, 1931 (R126)

From 1697 until 1887 the Pavement end of the Shambles was dominated by the Italianate tower of St Crux's church, described by Francis Drake in 1736 as 'a handsome new steeple of brick coined with stone'. Robert Davies, however, in 1859, was to put an opposite view: 'the unsightly cupola, and its tower of brick, which now deforms the church of St Crux, bespeaks a tasteless . . . period'. This change in attitude by Victorian times, coupled with falling congregations in the City-centre churches, led to the 'destruction of something of distinction and beauty' in 1887. The absence of urns on the corners of the parapet, still there in 1845 when Fox Talbot photographed the church, hints at a third reason — the unsafe condition of the tower. Prior to total demolition, the tower had lost its cupola in 1872, nine years before the artist recorded it in this view!

81

Thomas White

St Crux's Church and Pavement, 1802

Pencil, watercolour and pen and ink
$12\frac{1}{8} \times 16\frac{3}{8}$ in (30.9 × 41.8 cm)
Signed and dated 1802 (on the reverse)
Purchased, 1938 (R230)

Worship ceased in St Crux's church in 1884, its parish was united with that of All Saints, Pavement, in 1885 and, although the conservationists made considerable efforts to save it, backed by the Society for the Preservation of Ancient Buildings, it was razed to the ground in 1887. For this, dynamite was necessary — leaving some doubt about the church's unsafeness, the prime reason for its demolition. Pavement, the site of one of the two general markets in York, Saturday Market, extended from St Crux to All Saints where a market cross, 'a Commendable piece of Architecture', was built. This was paid for out of £400 left in 1668 by Marmaduke Rawdon, son of a York alderman, to buy and pull down the houses next to the church; their materials were 'to be put toward making a Crosse or shelter for the markett people that sell meale and corne'. It was pulled down in 1813 to make more space for stalls.

82

Patrick Hall

Pavement with All Saints' Church, 1943

Pencil, black crayon and pen and ink
$9\frac{3}{4} \times 9\frac{1}{4}$ in (24.7 × 23.5 cm)
Signed and dated 1943
Possibly purchased from Henry Rushbury, 1946 (R3190)

During the Second World War a number of static water tanks were placed at strategic places throughout the City to provide an emergency supply of water for fire-fighting should the water mains be damaged by enemy bombing. One of these stood, conveniently out of the way, on the traffic roundabout that had been built at the junction of Pavement, Piccadilly and Parliament Street shortly after the closure of the electric tramway system in November 1935. After the War the roundabout gained a formally-planted flower bed but subsequently they were both removed.

83

Henry Cave

Entrance to the White Swan Inn, Pavement, 1811

Etching
7⅞ × 6 in (20 × 15.2 cm)
Signed
Published by Henry Cave, York, 1811
Transferred from the Castle Museum, 1976
(R2276)

When Piccadilly was constructed in 1911, a range of jettied houses in Pavement was pulled down. Behind these houses was a yard, surrounded by the buildings of the White Swan Inn, a noted coaching house and York terminus for coaches from Sheffield, Leeds, Newcastle, Oldham and Liverpool. The inn was also demolished, to be rebuilt later on the west side of the new street. The jetty above its Pavement doorway had been supported by two ornately-carved oak brackets, 'the enrichments and singular fancies of an early period' and above them was displayed the name of the landlord since June 1784, John Hardcastle, who had moved to the White Swan from the Bay Horse, Jubbergate. After his death in March 1800 he was succeeded by his son, Thomas.

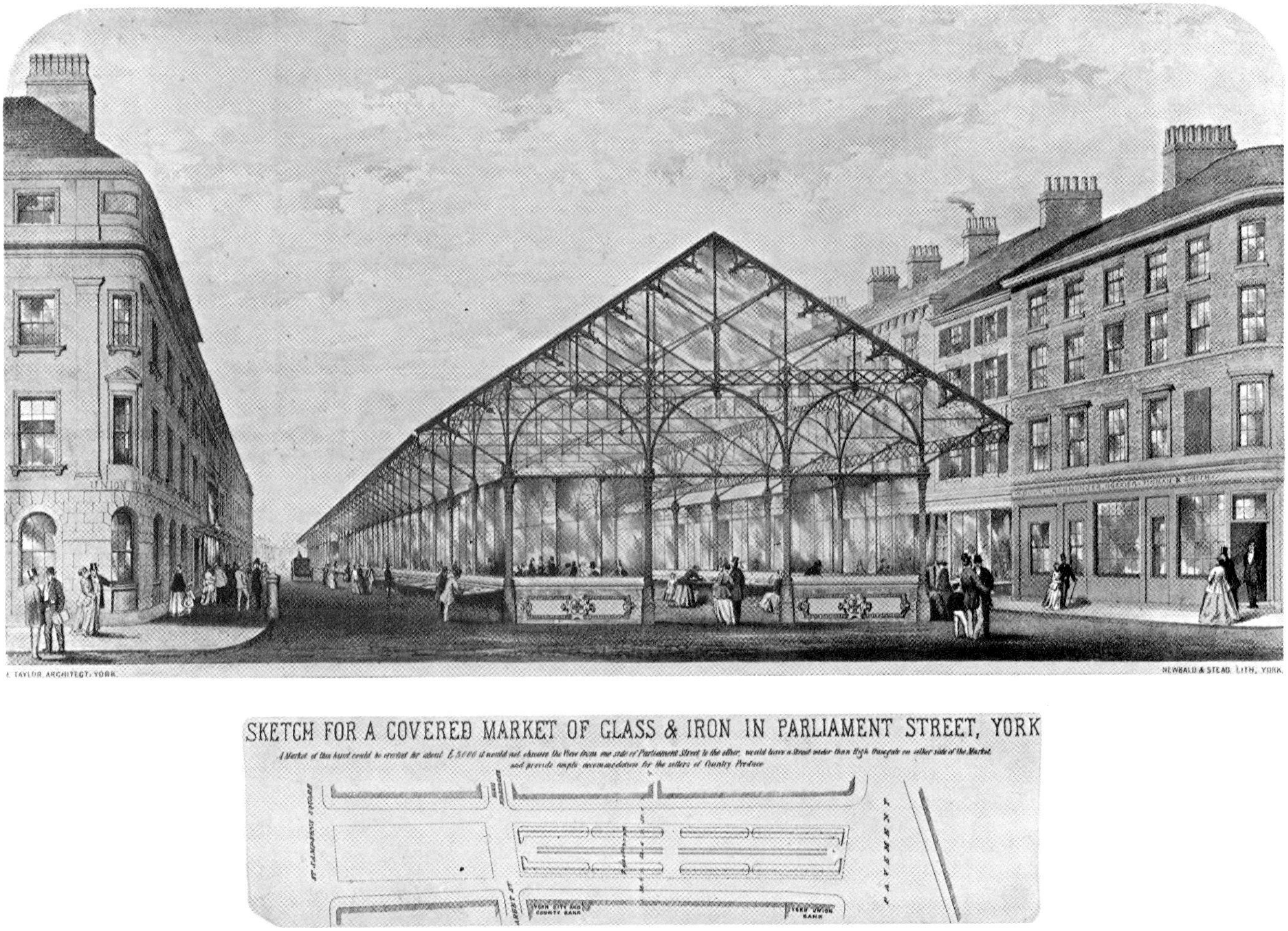

84

Edward Brown
after Edward Taylor

'Sketch for a Covered Market of Glass & Iron in Parliament Street, York', *c.* 1853

Colour lithograph
$13\frac{1}{4} \times 26\frac{1}{2}$ in (33.6×67.5 cm), image
Printed by Newbald & Stead, York
Provenance unknown (R2838)

Despite the demolition of Thursday Market cross there was still insufficient space in the markets for the traders wishing to bring their wares for sale in the City. In 1827, therefore, the Corporation obtained an Act of Parliament for the construction of a new and spacious street between St Sampson's Square and Pavement. Here the new market opened on 16 June 1836 with 185 stalls selling food and general goods. But still the traders were not satisfied: having gained the extra space they now required protection from the weather. Proposals were made in 1853 to erect a covered stand the length of Parliament Street. One plan was submitted by Edward Taylor, who was eventually to design the building which is now the Art Gallery, but after much discussion nothing came of this scheme nor others proposed in 1863 and 1869. Finally, in 1871, the problem was resolved by the provision of movable covered stalls with iron supports and wooden gratings for the stall-holders to stand on.

85

Francis Bedford

St Sampson's Church, 1843

Two-toned lithograph
$6\frac{5}{8} \times 9$ in (17×22.7 cm), image
Signed
Purchased as part of the Evelyn Collection, 1931 (R1923)

In medieval times sea fish was sold on Foss Bridge and freshwater fish on King's Staithe. These specialist markets moved to Pavement and St Sampson's Square, respectively, in the late eighteenth century but a new fish market with a market cross was opened in 1837 in Silver Street adjacent to St Sampson's church, as an annex to the new Parliament Street market. The first mention of this church is in 1154 but its building was totally replaced by the end of the fifteenth century. Because of the deterioration of its fabric it was closed and almost totally rebuilt between 1845 and 1848, re-using or copying its medieval features. The top stage of the tower was removed at the same time and not replaced until 1909. It was closed as a parish church in 1968 and has, since 1974, enjoyed a new lease of life as an old people's 'social centre in the City of York for rest, refreshment, leisure and companionship'.

86

Unidentified Artist

Old Market Building, St Sampson's Square, 1736

Engraving
$5\frac{1}{2} \times 5\frac{1}{4}$ in (14.1 × 13.3 cm)
Provenance unknown (R2417)

Over the centuries York has had a number of single-commodity markets, located at various sites throughout the City, and two general markets — Saturday Market in Pavement and Thursday Market in St Sampson's Square. In the centre of Thursday Market a stone cross, a shelter for the market traders in bad weather 'set upon an ascent of five steps, round which was a penthouse supported by eight wooden pillars', was built with twenty marks left in 1421 in the will of the widow of John Braythwayt, a past mayor. A standard yard-measure for the sale of cloth was fixed to one of the pillars in 1593. The cross was replaced in 1704 by a much larger building on the west side of the square, 'a beautiful and useful structure'. This in turn was demolished in 1815 to make space for market stalls, a victim of commercial pressure.

87

Dennis Flanders

The Guildhall after War Damage, 1942

Pencil, charcoal and wash
22 × 16½ in (56 × 42 cm)
Signed and dated 1942
Purchased from the artist, 1942 (R2480)

On 29 April 1942 York suffered its worst air raid of eleven in the Second World War when the city was specifically selected as a target in part reprisal for British raids on medieval Lubeck on 28 and 29 March. During a period of two hours sixty-five high-explosive bombs and fourteen clusters of incendiary bombs were dropped. Seventy-nine people were killed and two hundred and four injured while many buildings were damaged or destroyed. One of these was the fifteenth-century Guildhall, reduced to a shell when incendiary bombs, caught on a platform erected in 1938 to enable timbers ravaged by the death-watch beetle to be replaced, set fire to its roof. Had not this platform been there, the bombs would have fallen on to the stone floor where they would have either burnt-out harmlessly or been extinguished by fire wardens. The new Guildhall, a faithful copy of the old and having risen phoenix-like out of its own ashes, was opened by the Queen Mother in 1960.

88

Attributed to
Thomas White

Coney Street with the Mansion House, *c.* 1800

Pencil, watercolour and pen and ink
12 × 16¼ in (30.6 × 41.3 cm)
Purchased as part of the Evelyn Collection, 1931 (R1556)

A clock was added to the east wall of St Martin, Coney Street, in 1668 but was replaced by a new one in 1778, bracketed-out over the street and surmounted by the figure of a naval officer fixing his position by sighting the sun with his cross-staff. In 1856 he was given a new quarter-deck on a third clock mounted on a new bracket. It had plate-glass dials with gold numerals, lit from within by gas turned on and off by an ingenious contrivance in the mechanism, all constructed by Thomas Cooke at his Buckingham Street works. From 1724 until gas lighting appeared in 1824 the streets were lit first by ninety-two oil lamps and later, in 1763, by over four hundred 'fixed with irons against the Walls of the Streets, Lanes and Publick Ways or upon strong Posts fit to support the same'. More elaborate lamps were placed in wrought-iron lamp-brackets over the doors of the best houses, including the Mansion House, the home of the Lord Mayor during his year of office since 1730.

89

George Nicholson

St Peter's Prison, 1837

Pencil and watercolour
$7^3/_8 \times 9^3/_8$ in (18.8 × 23.7 cm)
Dated 3 October 1837
Acquired by 1934 (R3029)

Johnathan Martin was apprehended in Hexham, his birthplace, on 6 February 1829 and sent to St Peter's Prison. From early times the Dean and Chapter had exercised jurisdiction in their liberty (which comprised areas in the City and eight counties) and had a gaol to imprison felons. Once in Minster Gates, it was eventually moved to a site just within Peter Gate, the entrance to the Minster Close from Lop Lane. In 1818 it was in a 'wretched state' and in 1836 the Inspector of Prisons found it 'without a single requisite for a prison'. Peter Gate had been pulled down in 1827 and the prison followed it in 1838, an indication that the Dean and Chapter's jurisdiction was over. Martin was detained there only for a few hours for examination by the magistrates of the liberty before being committed to the City Gaol to await trial.

The Minster Area

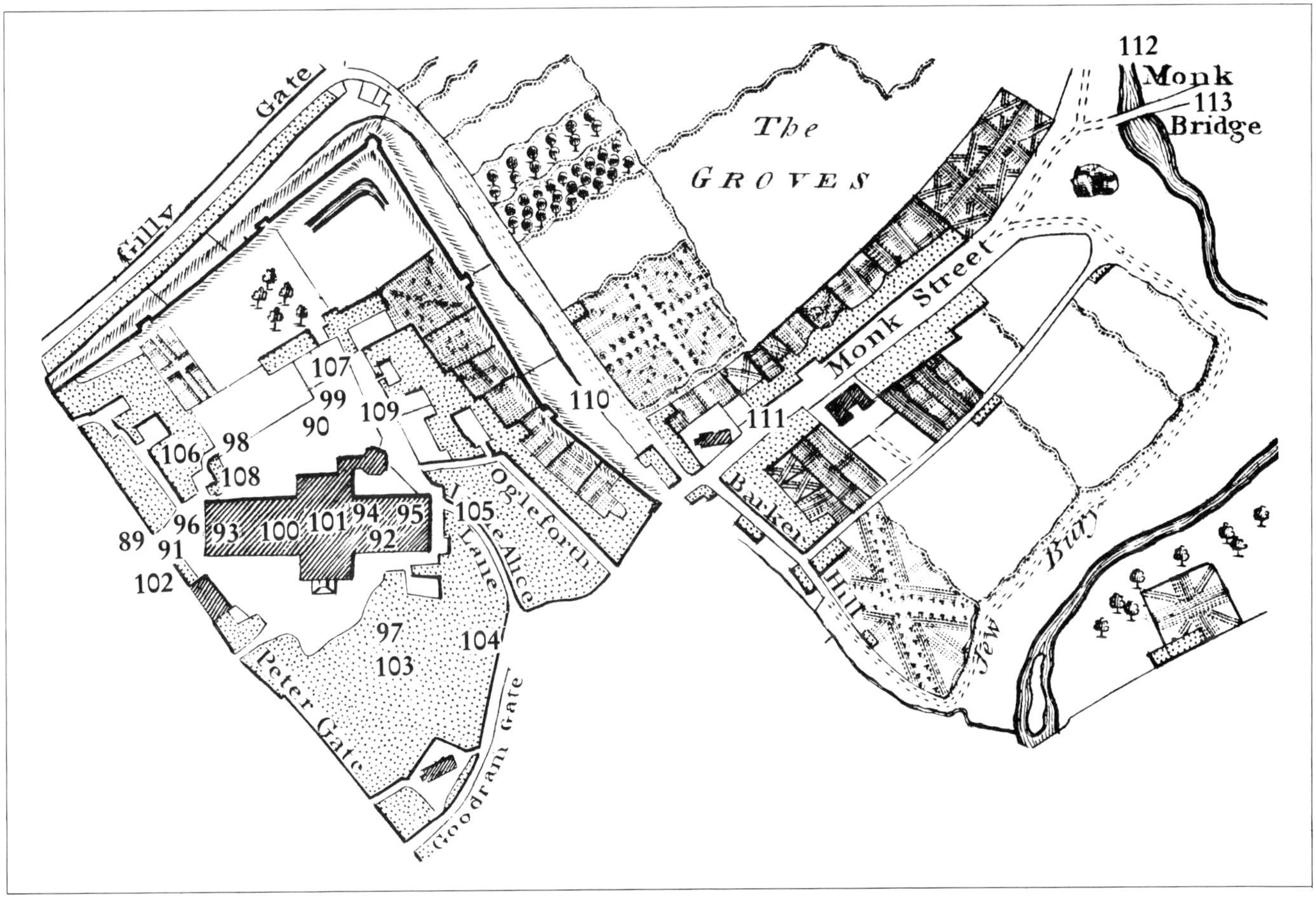

90

Joseph Nutting
after Edmond Barker

'North-East Prospect of the Cathedral Church of York', 1716

Etching
$20\frac{1}{2} \times 31$ in (52.1×78.7 cm)
Sold by Thomas Marsh, Minster Gates, York
Provenance unknown (R1474)

Between 1666 and 1808 the lantern tower of the Minster was surmounted by a hexagonal gazebo. This was built, at the order of George Villiers, Duke of Buckingham, Lord Lieutenant of the West Riding and the City of York, to house a beacon to alarm the citizens of an invasion by the Dutch or the French, with whom the country was then at war. It was constructed in wood, glazed, covered in lead and surmounted by a cockerel-shaped vane. This was not the crest of the Duke of Buckingham but a symbol to represent Peter, patron saint of the Minster, to whom Christ had said: 'I tell thee Peter, the cock shall not crow this day, before that thou shalt thrice deny that thou knowest me.'

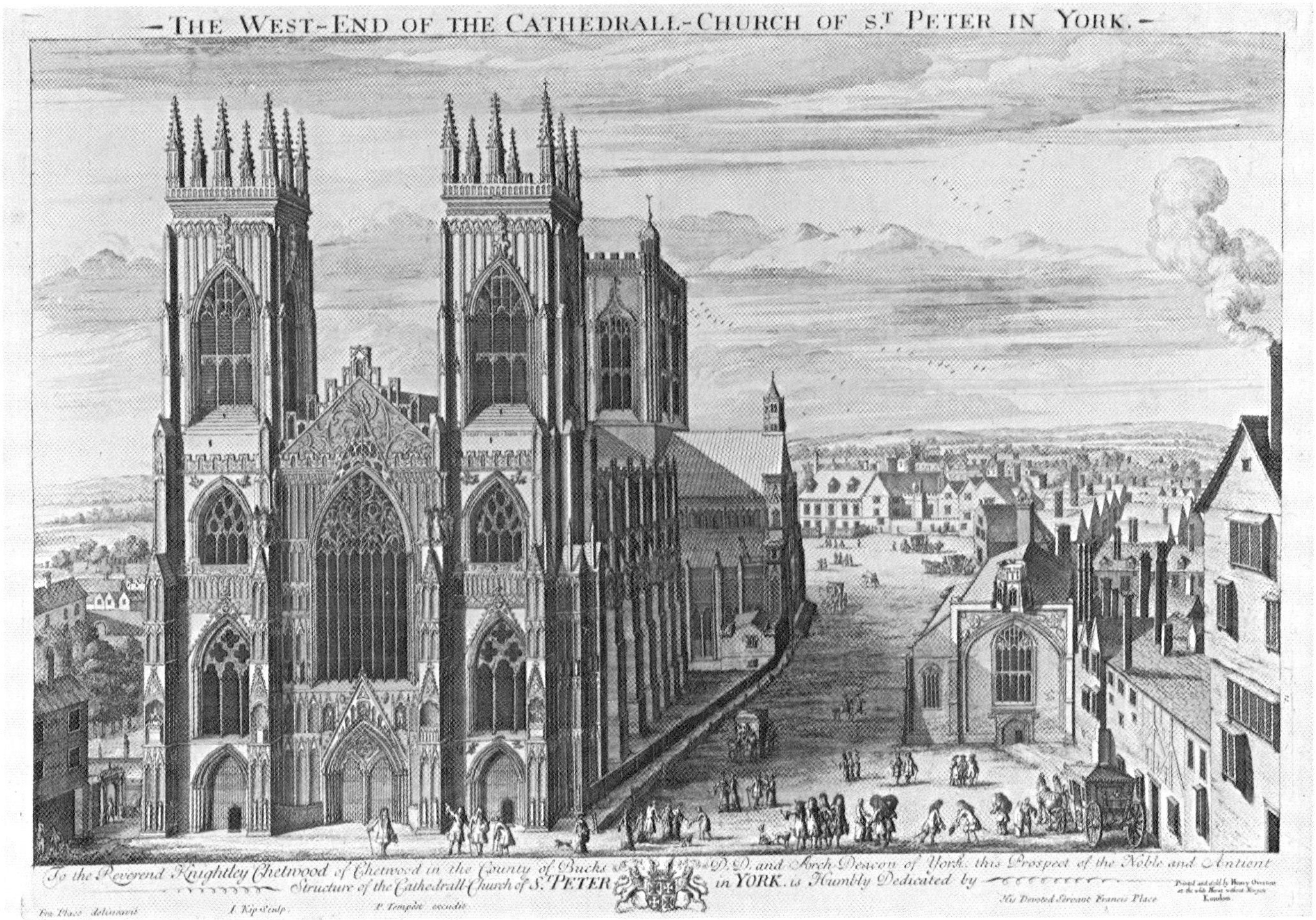

91

Jan Kip and Pierce Tempest
after Francis Place

'The West-End of the Cathedrall Church of St Peter in York', 1730

Etching
17⅛ × 24⅞ in (43.5 × 63.3 cm)
Printed and sold by Henry Overton at the White Horse without Newgate, London
Purchased as part of the Evelyn Collection, 1931 (R1555)

In the seventeenth century the west front of the Minster was obscured by 'certaine Houses built on either side close upon the wall' while 'meane Tenements' had been erected against the south transept. Charles I, in 1633, objected to 'that great abuse in buildeing Houses and Stables, with their uncleane passages, a great deale too neare to the house of God . . .' He forbade the erection of any more buildings adjacent to the Minster and renewal of the leases of those existing. In the last years of the seventeenth century Dean Thomas Gale 'pulled down the houses and cleaned this part of the church from the scurf it had contracted by the smoke proceeding from these buildings'.

92

John Haynes

Interior of Minster, looking East, 1735

Pencil, grey wash, pen and black ink and watercolour
$14\frac{3}{8} \times 16\frac{7}{8}$ in (36.5 × 42.8 cm)
Purchased, 1983 (R2384)

Celia Fiennes, touring England on horseback, visited York in 1697 and recorded in her journal that 'the body of the Church is large . . . all these Isles are broad, the people of fashion use them to walke in and on that account its much [pity] that they keep it not cleaner'. The broken surface of the floor, a muddle of gravestones, many without their 'splendid brass adornments', must have contributed to the lack of cleanliness. A proposal in 1730 to take up the old floor and replace it with one designed by Lord Burlington and his associate William Kent met with a generous public response. Work started in 1735 using white stone from a quarry at Huddlestone, given by Sir Edward Gascoigne, relieved by a regular pattern in blue marble. The latter came from both the floor of St Martin, Coney Street (exchanged by its churchwardens for some of the old floor) and Mr Wilberforce of Hull.

93

Joseph Halfpenny

Scaffolding at the West End of the Minster, 1796

Pencil, watercolour and pen and ink
$18\frac{3}{4} \times 24\frac{3}{8}$ in (47.7 × 61.8 cm)
Probably purchased, 1943 (R1784)

In *c.* 1793 it was decided to clean and paint the entire interior of the Minster as 'the whole of the gilded key-knots in the vaults, and gilded ribs, with every other decorated part of the vaults and walls, even the beautiful marble columns, imposts, and stringcourses, were either painted or coated with a body of lime and ochre, and all remnants of former embellishment were totally obliterated'. While the scaffolding was in place for this work Joseph Halfpenny made drawings of many of the vault bosses and other ornamentation which was otherwise inaccessible. He used many of these drawings to illustrate *Gothic Ornaments in the Cathedral Church of York* which he published in 1795. This view shows the groinings of the vault as they appeared before the spaces were closed with lath and plaster. No. 93 and the drawings and engravings made for *Gothic Ornaments* are of special historical importance because of the destruction caused by the Minster fires of 1829 and 1840.

94

Charles Wild

The Choir of the Minster, c. 1827

Pencil, watercolour and pen and ink
18½ × 14¼ in (47.1 × 36 cm)
Purchased as part of the Evelyn Collection, 1931 (R2726)

Wild himself, writing in 1809, described the choir as 'incomparably richer [than the nave] in the decorative parts, as would necessarily arise from its later erection and superior sanctity . . . The stalls in the choir are uncommonly rich, and well carved in oak; the principal seats, as anciently, without exception, turn up to form what are called misericords, or half seats, which were used for penitential inclinations. Many of them are ornamented with very singular devices, alluding to the ignorance or irregularity of the secular clergy. But the workmanship is everywhere well executed. . . . The pulpit, cathedra [bishop's seat], and their pews, are from the design of Kent, and surprisingly incorrect, as he did not consider the model the [medieval] stalls afforded him'. All this woodwork was destroyed in the 1829 fire.

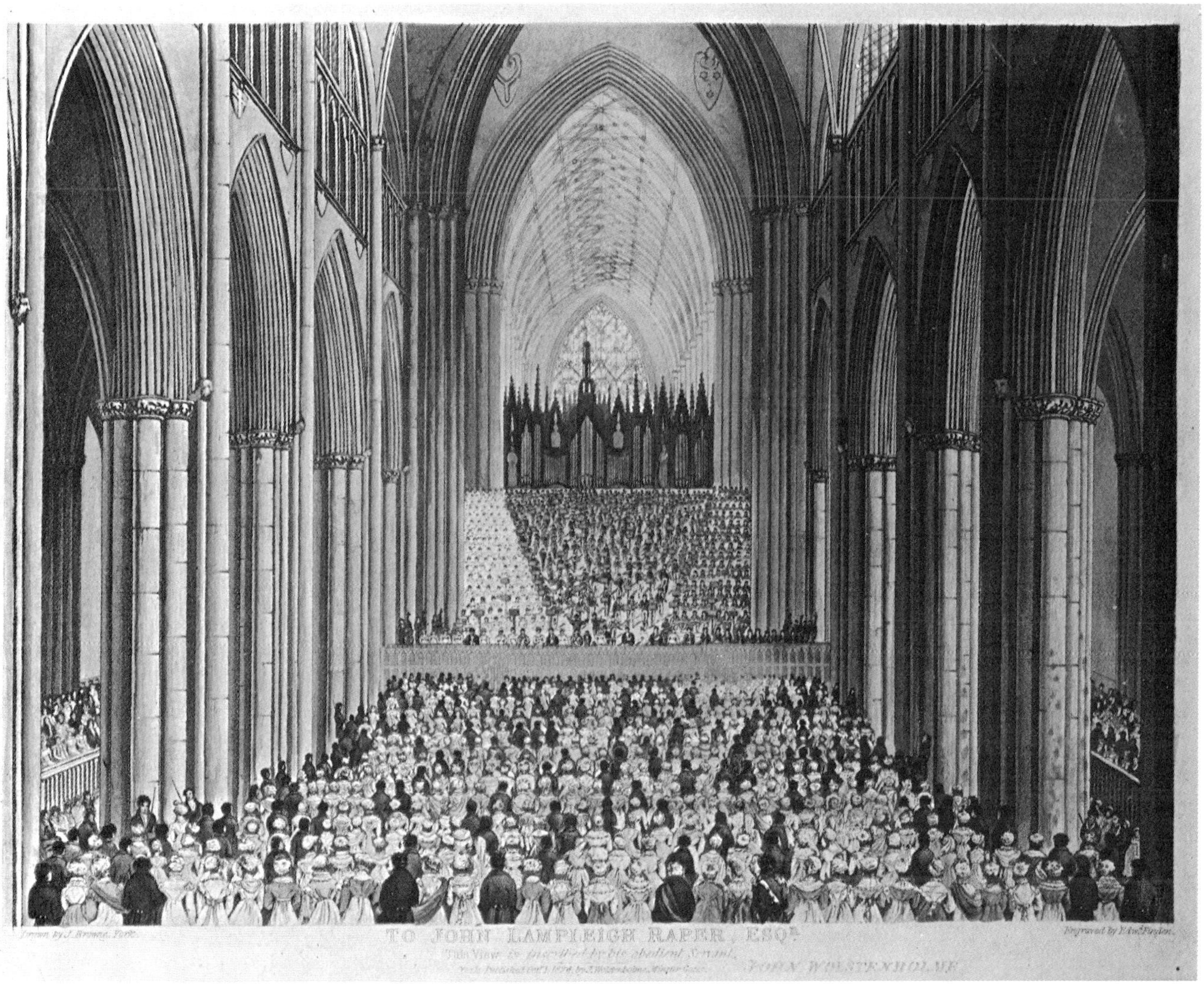

95

Edward Finden
after John Brown(e)

York Music Festival, 1824

Etching, aquatint and watercolour
$8\frac{3}{4} \times 11\frac{3}{8}$ in (22.2 × 28.9 cm)
Published by J. Wolstenholme, Minster Gates, York, 1 October 1824
Purchased as part of the Evelyn Collection, 1931 (R1460)

Although a festival had been held in the Minster in 1791 it was not until 1823 that the event benefited charities, an objective first instituted at a meeting of the three choirs of Gloucester, Worcester and Hereford in 1724. The Dean and Chapter gave permission for the cathedral to be used for a four-day festival to raise funds for the York County Hospital and the Hull, Leeds and Sheffield General Infirmaries. A vast number of performers was assembled: a chorus of sixty-four trebles, fifty-four altos, seventy-five tenors and seventy-nine basses together with an orchestra of sixty-six violins, twenty violas, twenty cellos, sixteen double-basses, fifty-three wind instruments and two drums as well as seventeen soloists and conductors. Their performances were described as magnificent. The nave seated 1,600 spectators and there was room in a gallery under the west window for a further 1,000. When the festival was over a profit of £7,200 had been achieved from takings of £16,140 and was distributed equally among the four hospitals.

96

Joseph Baker

'The South-West Prospect of the Cathedral Church of York', c. 1750

Pencil, grey wash, bodycolour and pen and black ink
20½ × 28½ in (52 × 72.5 cm)
Provenance unknown (R1806)

In 1907 the Minster stonemasons completed the work of building flying buttresses on the nave clerestory. When G. F. Bodley, architect to the Dean and Chapter, who thought they had been part of the original design, proposed, in 1898, to add them to the building he started a long-running controversy. The architectural press thought them 'a useless absurdity' as the wooden roof and vault did not need their support, but Dean Purey-Cust regarded the evidence for their previous existence, the ragged condition of the bases of the pinnacles and toothing in the nave wall, as incontrovertible. Besides, 'What Gothic building approaching the size of the Minster is lacking of them ?' he wrote, more emotionally, in 1905. He had found 'no less than seven old prints in the Minster Library, one dated 1750, shewing . . . flying buttresses existing on the south side'. If this is firm evidence for their existence in 1750 it is surprising that no contemporary evidence exists for their later removal.

97

John Hunter

The Minster, 'Taken on the spot from the South-East corner of Dr Hunter's Garden', 1784

Pencil, watercolour and pen and ink
16½ × 21¼ in (41.9 × 53.9 cm)
Signed and dated 1784
Purchased, 1938 (R2203)

In 1876, during a restoration of the south transept that was to contribute considerably to its survival in the fire of 9 July 1984, G. E. Street, architect to the Dean and Chapter, decided to remove the pinnacle surmounted by the statue of the little fiddler and the two drum towers from the end of the transept. After experimenting with full-size wooden models he replaced them with a cross on the ridge and two pinnacles at the sides. From early times until 1831 the deans of York had lived in a house to the south of the Minster. The Old Deanery which had passed into private hands during the Commonwealth, was replaced by a large stone house in the Gothic style on the north side of the Minster. This was in turn demolished in 1940 when the present Deanery was built. In place of the Old Deanery a new building, now the Minster Song School, was erected in 1833 for St Peter's School.
Dr Hunter's house stood next to the Old Deanery grounds, and is now occupied by the York College for Girls.

98

Paul Sandby Munn

The West Towers of the Minster, 1810

Pencil and watercolour
$13\frac{7}{8} \times 10\frac{3}{4}$ in (35.7×27.2 cm)
Purchased, 1952 (R1862)

After 250 years of work the Minster was finally consecrated on 3 July 1472, upon the completion of the western towers. Following the death, in 1420, of William Colchester, who had been sent by the King to supervise the rebuilding of the lantern tower after its collapse in 1407, it was decided not to complete his design for a bell chamber above the lantern. Instead work began, in 1433, on a new tower for the bells at the south-west corner, followed by a matching north-west tower. The precinct of the Archbishop's Palace on the north side of the Minster, of which only the chapel (now the Minster Library) and a cloister arcade remain, was entered through a gatehouse attached to the north aisle of the nave. This gatehouse and the building next to it, part of Sir Arthur Ingram's mansion, were pulled down in 1816.

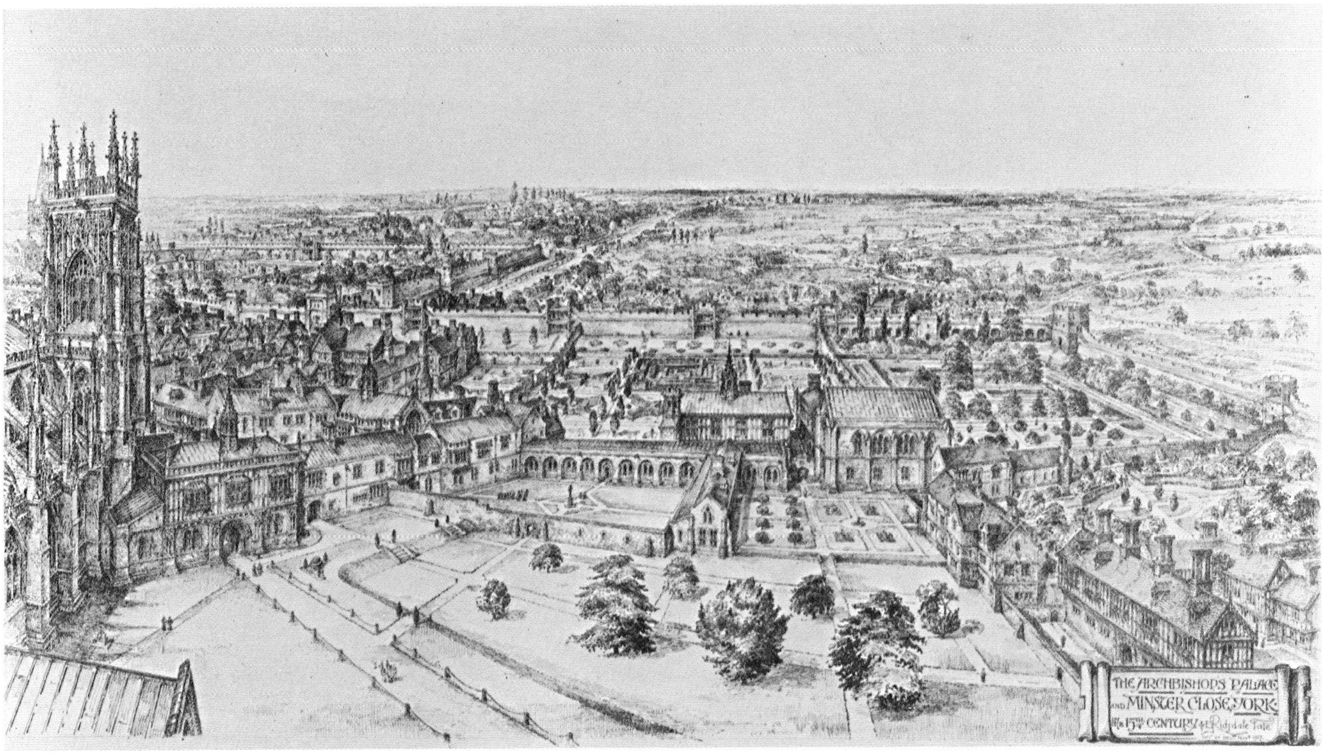

99

Edwin Ridsdale Tate

The Archbishop's Palace and Minster Close in the fifteenth Century, 1917

Pencil, pen and black ink
14⅞ × 22 in (37.9 × 68.6 cm), image
Signed and dated November 1917
Purchased as part of the Evelyn Collection, 1931 (R2331)

The Archbishop's Palace on the north side of the Minster was probably started by Roger of Pont L'Evêque at the end of the twelfth century. All that now remains of its extensive buildings is part of the arcade of the original cloister and a chapel built in the next century. Other parts survived, however, until 1816 when the gatehouse and the ruins of Sir Arthur Ingram's house were demolished. The decline of the palace started when Archbishop Young, with 'avaricious desire', sold the lead from the roof of the great hall in the 1560s. The ruins of the palace were granted to Sir Arthur Ingram in 1616. He built a mansion, where he was to entertain Charles I in 1642, adjacent to the gatehouse at the north-west corner of the Minster. He laid out the rest of the site as pleasure gardens with 'a pleasant fair Tennis-Court, a delightful large bowling ground . . . [and] curiously contrived Fish-ponds'.

100

John Brown(e)

'View of the Interior of York Minster. As it appeared immediately after the Roof fell in on the morning of the 2nd February, 1829', 1829

Lithograph
$12\frac{3}{8} \times 9\frac{3}{8}$ in (31.4 × 23.8 cm)
Printed by Engelmann, Graf, Coindet & Co.
Published by Rudolph Ackermann & Co., Repository of Arts, 96 Strand, London, 12 March 1829
Purchased as part of the Evelyn Collection, 1931 (R2597)

On 1 February 1829 Jonathan Martin, a tanner with a vocation to reform the Church of England on Methodist principles and to warn its clergy against their sins, attended evensong in the Minster. He thought the congregation insincere and 'the organ made such a noise of buzz! buzz!'. He said to himself 'I'll have thee down tonight, thou shalt buzz no more' and, after the service, hid behind the tomb of Archbishop Greenfield until the verger had locked up. Emerging from his hiding place he made two piles of books and cushions in the choir stalls, set light to them and then escaped by cutting a hole through a window. The fire burned unnoticed through the night and was seen only next morning when a choir boy called Swinbank fell over while skating in Minster Yard and, looking up, saw smoke pouring from a nave window. When he gave the alarm the Minster staff tried in vain to subdue the flames with the Minster fire engine.

101

John Brown(e)

'A Representation of the Choir of York Minster, as it appeared from the Organ Screen, on the 3rd of February 1829. The day after the Fire', 1829

Lithograph
$12\frac{1}{8} \times 9\frac{3}{8}$ in (30.7×23.8 cm), image
Printed by Charles Hullmandel.
Published by Rudolph Ackermann & Co., Repository of Arts, 96 Strand, London, 12 March 1829
Purchased as part of the Evelyn Collection, 1931 (R2598)

After a long interval two City fire engines appeared on the scene but the firemen were 'old and incapacitated . . . and were of little use'. The Yorkshire Insurance Company's engine was next to arrive, followed by one from the Cavalry Barracks but the fire had too great a hold and the choir roof crashed down as the Minster clock struck nine. Further engines arrived — Beilby Thompson's private engine drawn by four greys, from Escrick, and one from Tadcaster. In the afternoon the town engine and three insurance-company engines from Leeds brought the total up to ten and the fire was under control by evening. The rest of the Minster was saved but the choir roof, sixty-six stalls, the archbishop's throne, the pulpit and the organ were destroyed. Martin was caught four days later and sentenced to life imprisonment. Restoration, for which a public subscription raised £49,619, started immediately and was completed by 6 May 1832. Bolting the stable door after the horse had gone, the Dean and Chapter reinstated the night watchman in the cathedral!

Printed by C Hullmandel

YORK MINSTER,
as it appeared on the Night of the Fire Wednesday the 20th May 1840

102

Unidentified Artist

'York Minster, as it appeared on the Night of the Fire, Wednesday, the 20th May, 1840', 1840

Two-toned lithograph
9 × 12⅜ in (22.9 × 31.4 cm), image
Printed by Charles Hullmandel
Published by J. W. Southgate, Library, 161 Strand, London, and William Hargrave, Library, Coney Street, York, 2 June 1840
Probably purchased, 1972 (R2611)

On 20 May 1840 William Groves, a clockmaker, was cleaning and repairing the clock in the bell-chamber in the south-west tower and 'having a candle, not enclosed as it ought to be in a lanthorne' fixed it in a hole in a piece of deal. When he finished he left the candle burning and it must have set light to debris, including relics of jackdaws' nests, and eventually burnt its way to the floor — thirty-five tons of wood saturated with oil and tallow. Some boys who saw a light in the belfrey gave the alarm at about 9 p.m. and three fire engines from the Yorkshire Insurance Company, which since 1830 had been responsible for fire-fighting in the City, and the North of England Insurance Company arrived very quickly. Further fire engines from Leeds (for which a special express train had been sent) together with those of the military and Bielby Thompson, now Lord Escrick, contained the fire to the nave thus saving the lantern tower, screen and the new organ.

103

William Monkhouse

'York Minster As it appeared from St Peter's School, on the night of the Fire (20th May 1840)', 1840

Colour lithograph
7⅛ × 9⅞ in (18.2 × 25.3 cm), image
Purchased as part of the Evelyn Collection, 1931 (R2610)

The York Operative Protestants' Association, meeting nearby, had refused to believe that the Minster was once again alight, thinking it a Roman Catholic hoax. Its members were soon disabused and joined the throng of spectators who saw the nave roof fall and the sudden glare of fire which lit up the great crucifix in the west window of the south aisle. The crucifix shone out 'distinct and beautiful, and the cordon of soldiers, which surrounded the building to keep back the crowds, involuntarily raised their right hands and saluted'. A second appeal within eleven years was greeted with less enthusiasm and raised only £21,591 towards the restoration, which was completed by 7 July 1844. The total cost of the two restorations was £105,560 and the portion not met by subscription was raised by realizing capital. Once again the Dean and Chapter belatedly closed a stable door when they decided to insure the Minster against fire – of no help for these two fires but invaluable in the aftermath of the 1984 fire!

104

Attributed to
Frederick Mackenzie

The Minster from the South-East, *c.* 1840

Pen, watercolour, pen and ink, and bodycolour
11⅝ × 16½ in (29.5 × 42.1 cm)
Purchased, 1946 (R1931)

In 1750 Henry Hindley installed 'an elegant and excellent clock' over the doorway to the south transept. This replaced the great medieval clock whose mechanism in the east aisle of the transept blocked one of the windows and was, by this time, 'ruinous and bad'. As the Minster clock was the one by which 'the inhabitants of the city chiefly regulate their hours', they were willing to contribute considerably to the cost of almost £300 for providing a new clock. It was removed in 1871, during the restoration of the south transept, and twelve years later, erected in its present position in the north transept with the two oak men-at-arms from its medieval predecessor to strike the four quarters.

105

Attributed to
Frederick Mackenzie

The Minster from the East, *c.* 1840

Pencil, watercolour, pen and ink, and bodycolour
11¼ × 16⅜ in (28.6 × 41.5 cm)
Provenance unknown (R216)

Even at its truncated height of 210 ft the lantern tower presents a formidable obstacle to some of the visitors who attempt the climb to its summit. Thomas Baskerville, who was in York in 1677, found, at the age of forty-seven, 'the stairs so high to get up and down that it made my thighs ache very much and I fell that night into a fever'. He could view the Archbishop's Palace at Bishopthorpe only from a distance as 'my travail to the top of the tower did so far discompose me that I could not go myself'. It is possible that it was intended to erect a spire on the central tower which, as it is, stands only a few feet higher than the western towers. Sir Nikolaus Pevsner thought this 'a pity, for equality of height does not make for a perfect composition from afar'.

106

Attributed to
Frederick Mackenzie

The Minster from the North-West, *c.* 1840

Pencil, watercolour, pen and ink, and bodycolour
11 × 16 in (28 × 40.8 cm)
Purchased, 1946 (R172)

The demolition of the houses against the west end and the south transept of York Minster was followed just over a century later by the removal of the gatehouse of the Archbishop's Palace and the remains of Sir Arthur Ingram's house in 1816. Thus an open space was created right round the cathedral. In the newly-cleared area on the north side a new deanery was built in 1831, standing in spacious grounds known at first as Deanery Park, but in more recent years as Dean's Park.

107

Moses Griffith

'St Sepulchre's Abbey' (actually the Chapel of the former Archbishop's Palace), 1777

Pencil, watercolour and pen and black ink, within the artist's original wash-line border
10 × 14⅛ in (25.4 × 35.9 cm), image
Signed and dated 13 June 1777
Purchased, 1947 (R127)

St Sepulchre's Chapel, the popular name of the chapel of St Mary and the Holy Angels, was built by Archbishop Roger in the twelfth century on an angle at the north-west corner of the Minster adjoining the gatehouse of the Archbishop's Palace. After the rebuilding of the nave it was entered from the Minster by a door still extant in the north aisle. The chapel, neglected after being made redundant in 1547, gradually disappeared until the last traces were swept away in 1816. Moses Griffith has confused this building with the thirteenth-century chapel of the Archbishop's Palace, here depicted, which was in 'derelict and disreputable' state after it had been abandoned in the sixteenth century. In 1810, repaired and converted by the Dean and Chapter, it became a new and more commodious home for the Minster Library, which from *c.* 1420 had been housed in a building between the south transept and the nave.

108

Henry Cave

'Back of the Minster', 1803

Pencil
8⅞ × 13 in (22.6 × 33.2 cm)
Signed and dated 1803
Purchased, 1938 (R2706)

In valuing the old buildings on the north side of the Minster in 1801 William Halfpenny, carpenter, and William Shout, mason, included a sum of £100 10*s*. for the Hole in the Wall, a tavern above the archbishop's prison behind the Palace gatehouse. The archbishop had had a prison by 1351, known to be within the Palace garth by 1385. After the sixteenth century the prison, possibly the crypt of St Sepulchre's Chapel, was no longer required and the building above became a public house. During its demolition in 1816 an underground room, fitted up with iron staples in the walls, iron shutters on the windows and oak stocks, was found underneath it. At one end, about five feet above the floor, was a cavity in the wall with steps leading up from it, probably the entrance to the prison. It was this cavity, thought for many years to have been used for immuring prisoners, which had given the public house its name.

109

Paul Hogarth

St George's Day in York, 1961

Pencil, watercolour and chalk
$24\frac{3}{8} \times 17$ in (62×43.3 cm)
Signed and dated 1961
Commissioned as the Evelyn Award, 1960
(R2207)

April 23, the feast day of the patron saint of England, is today marked by a parade of Scouts and Guides taking part in a service in the Minster but, before the Reformation, there was a riding of St George in procession, presented by the religious guild of St Christopher and St George. The festivities on this day also included the performance of a play. The custom was revived in 1554 and repeated every year until 1557 but it was not to survive the change in religious attitudes brought about by the death of Mary and the accession of Elizabeth.

110

Henry Cave

Monk Bar and Lord Mayor's Walk, 1803

Pencil
9⅝ × 10⅝ in (24.4 × 26.9 cm)
Transferred from the Castle Museum, 1975
(R3077)

The original Monkgate lay on the line of the Roman road from Monk Bridge to the *porta decumana* of the fortress in Lord Mayor's Walk, where its site is marked by remains of a former tower and rebuilding of the wall. When the stone defences were being constructed in the fourteenth century a new gate was built on the present site and the street name transferred to the new road. The rooms in the bar were used as a prison, called Little Ease, during the sixteenth century, and more recently, from 1845 to 1913, were the home of a police inspector. The moat, which once formed part of the City's defences, has largely disappeared under buildings and car parks, except for a stretch in Lord Mayor's Walk, formerly Goose Lane, whose survival was ensured by its use, until the 1930s, as a field by a farm on the Gillygate corner.

111

Thomas Shotter Boys

Monkgate and Monk Bar, with the Entrance to old St Maurice's Churchyard, *c.* 1840

Pencil and sepia ink
8¾ × 11⅝ in (22.4 × 29.5 cm)
Purchased as part of the Evelyn Collection, 1931 (R266)

Travellers entering York by Monkgate, a broad street for most of its length, were funnelled by St Maurice's churchyard into the narrow arch of Monk Bar. The passage into the City was improved by the removal of part of the barbican in 1815 and the rest in 1825. It was further improved by the construction of a small arch on the Lord Mayor's Walk side in 1845 and a large arch on the other side in 1861, when part of the churchyard was sacrificed for road widening. The small twelfth-century church of St Maurice itself was pulled down in 1875 and replaced with a much larger Victorian edifice to cater for the expanding population in the newly-built suburbs outside the walls. As the suburbs grew further and further this church eventually found itself in the wrong place and, with a falling congregation, was demolished in 1967.

112

Unidentified Artist

The Minster from the Foss, *c.* 1800

Pencil, pen and ink, and watercolour
$7^1/_8 \times 9^7/_8$ in (18.1 × 25.2 cm), image
Provenance unknown (R3162)

The demise of the three-arched bridge was signalled by an indictment served against the Corporation by the Crown in 1791, because of its bad state of repair. The Corporation was saved some expense by the Foss Navigation Company, formed in 1793 to canalize the Foss between York and Sheriff Hutton, who paid a hundred pounds towards the cost of a new bridge with extra headroom and width as well as a towpath through it. Peter Atkinson the elder designed the new bridge which was built in 1794 but not without some misfortune. In November 1794 the old bridge collapsed during demolition: the keystone gave way and Thomas Day, who had a pregnant wife and three children, was killed. A public subscription was raised to provide some help for his destitute family. By 1926 the bridge, an obstruction to road traffic, was widened by a concrete structure on the downstream side and new parapets on both sides, but the remains of Atkinson's bridge can still be seen from beneath.

113

Ascribed to William Payne

The Minster from Monk Bridge, *c.* 1790

Etching and watercolour
6¾ × 10 in (17.2 × 25.6 cm)
Probably purchased, 1939 (R359)

Monk Bridge is built where the Roman road to Malton crossed the Foss. A bridge would not have been necessary before the river was dammed by the Normans in 1069, raising its level by 12ft 6in. However, no mention of it can be found until 1353 when Adam de Hibernia left 12*d*. in his will to the Maison Dieu, near Monk Bridge. When John Leland visited the City in 1534 he noted 'Monke bridge on Fosse of 5. arches withoute Goodrome gate' but this bridge, made of wood, was demolished in 1644 by the defenders of York to impede the Parliamentary forces. It was reconstructed in 1646 in stone with three arches. At the end of the eighteenth century the road beyond it, leading to Monk Bar, was already lined with houses, providing an early example of ribbon development.

The Castle Area

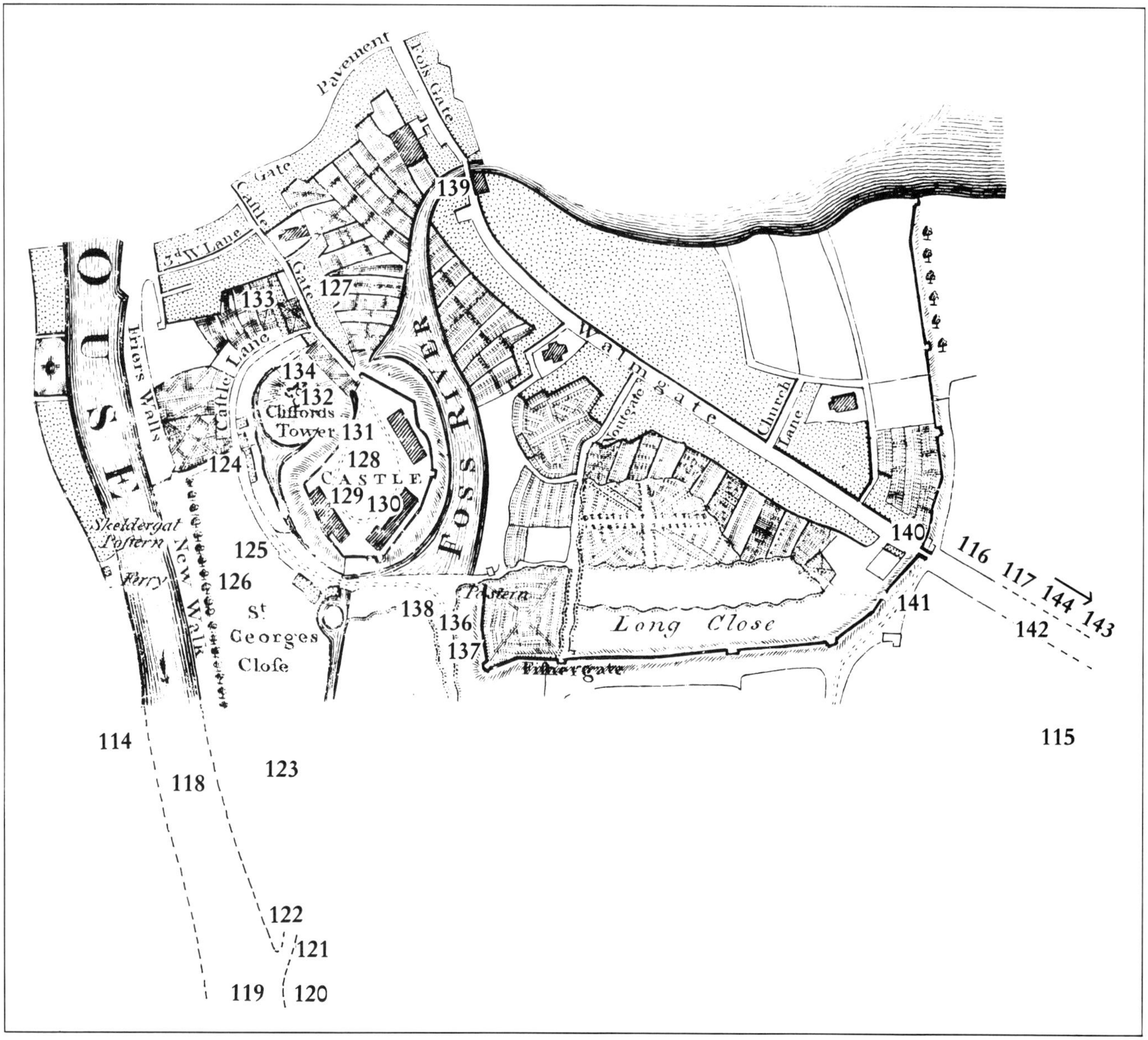

114

Edwin Ridsdale Tate

York in the fifteenth Century, 1914

Pencil, watercolour and pen and black ink
$19\frac{7}{8} \times 42\frac{3}{4}$ in (50.5 × 108.5 cm), image
Signed and dated 15 May 1914
Lent from the Mansion House (presented by Dr W. A. Evelyn on the occasion of the opening of the *Exhibition of 'Old York' Views*, 1927)

To see how York looked in the fifteenth century it is necessary to turn to a conjectural representation such as this. The medieval city, contained within its walls for most of the circumference, is further protected by water — a moat below the ramparts of the walls and the King's Fishpool in the Foss, already silting up and forming islands, in the east between Layerthorpe Postern and the Red Tower. The forty parish churches pale into insignificance amongst the great pre-reformation religious houses, which were as follows: the Benedictine Abbey of St Mary outside the walls in the north; St Leonard's Hospital run by brothers who lived by the rule of Austin Canons in a corner of the walls by the Roman Multangular Tower; the Priory of the Alien Benedictines in Micklegate; an Augustinian friary between Lendal and the Ouse; a Carmelite friary in the Hungate area; and a Franciscan friary on the east bank of the Ouse just to the north of Clifford's Tower.

115

Francis Place

York from the Windmill without Castlegate Postern, c. 1700

Pencil, pen and ink, and watercolour
4¾ × 9¾ in (12.2 × 24.6 cm)
Provenance unknown (R1811)

As the traveller approached York from Fulford at the end of the seventeenth century he was confronted by a panorama of the City dominated by the Minster in the centre. This rose above the gateway of the Castle, flanked by two great drum towers, and the Sessions Court in the Castle bailey. To the left of the Minster between the spires of St Mary, Castlegate, and All Saints, North Street (York's two surviving medieval spires) could be seen Clifford's Tower, standing high on its motte, and then the towers of St Michael, Spurriergate, St Martin, Coney Street, and St Olave, Marygate. On the right were the towers of St Denys and St Margaret, Walmgate. This skyline could still be seen today were it not for the suburban sprawl of the expanding City that grew up outside the walls in the nineteenth and twentieth centuries.

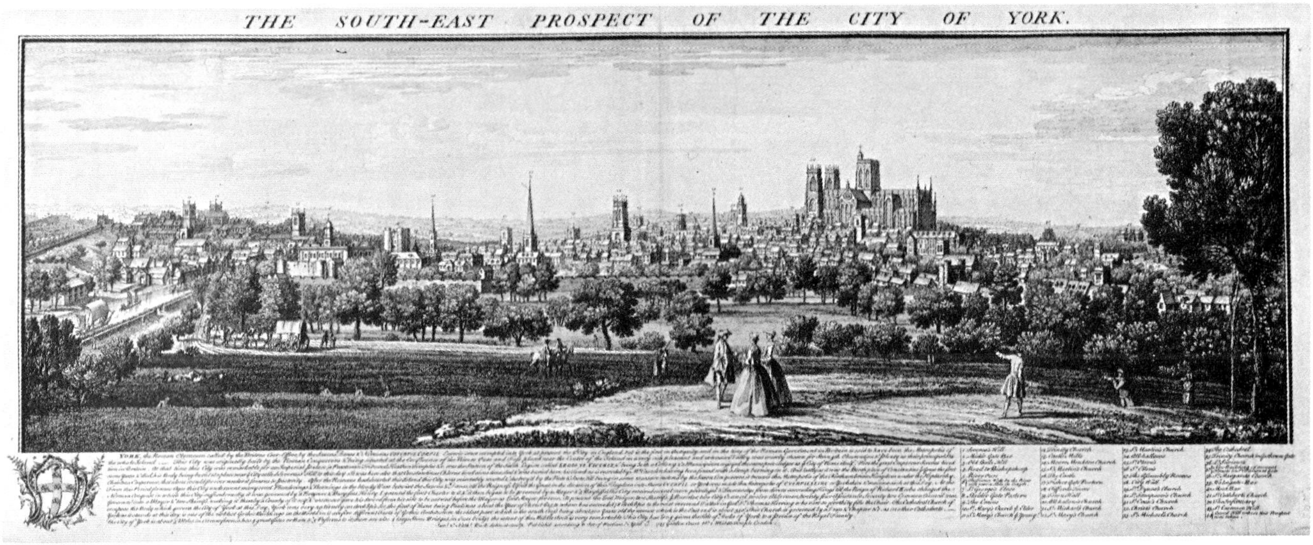

116 *(Above)*

Samuel and Nathaniel Buck

'The South-East Prospect of the City of York', 1743

Pencil, grey wash and pen and black ink
$12\frac{1}{4} \times 31$ in (31 × 78.9 cm)
Dated 1743
Purchased, 1939 (R3181)

This prospect is twenty-five years later than Barker's from the same viewpoint (No. 144) but the City appears largely unchanged. The church towers and spires all still appear in the same relative positions, although a terrace of large new houses has been built in St Saviourgate behind St Saviour's Church.

117 *(Below)*

Samuel and Nathaniel Buck

'The South-East Prospect of the City of York', 1745

Etching and engraving
$12\frac{3}{8} \times 31\frac{7}{8}$ in (31.4 × 81.2 cm)
Published 15 April 1745
Purchased as part of the Evelyn Collection, 1931 (R1782)

118

William Henry Toms
after Peter Monamy

'A South West View of the City of York', 1736

Etching and engraving
11⅞ × 14⅞ in (30.2 × 37.9 cm)
Published 1736
Provenance unknown (R3159)

From the confluence of the rivers Ouse and Foss an unobstructed view could be had along the Ouse, in 1736, to the old Ouse Bridge, as recorded here. On the east bank St George's Field, a narrow spit of land between the two rivers, was defined by a row of coniferous trees on the Foss side and the newly-planted limes and elms of the New Walk on the Ouse side (although the artist has depicted many more than the 130 bought by the Corporation to make this walk). The number of ships attempting to reach the City stresses the importance of the river to York as a trading artery, but two heeling over at their moorings off King's Staithe and others at anchor in the foreground indicate the problems of navigating a tidal river.

119

Francis Place

'York from near the Confluence of the Rivers Ouse and Foss', 1703

Pencil, brown wash, pen and sepia ink
$7\frac{1}{8} \times 12\frac{5}{8}$ in (18 × 32.3 cm)
Dated 1703
Purchased as part of the Evelyn Collection, 1931 (R1978)

Before 1757 ships navigating the Ouse from the Humber had to contend with the tides and numerous shoals in the river bed. This, coupled with a winding course and the lack of wind in the high-banked, tree-lined river, meant that shipmasters had often to rely on gangs of labourers to tow them to the City-centre staithes. Many proposals to improve the river were discussed by the Corporation, including a bold scheme to construct a direct tidal channel from Broomfleet to Fulford. The construction of a weir and the first of the two locks now at Naburn in 1857 raised the water level upstream of the dam by 4ft 6in and improved the last stage of the navigation but downstream with altered tidal flow, silt deposits built up and often impeded the passage of ships for long periods. The navigation authority, York Corporation, did little to improve the situation, thereby contributing greatly to the City's decline by the beginning of the nineteenth century.

120

Charles Grignion after Nathan Drake

'Prospect of a Noble Terras Walk', 1756

Etching and engraving
17½ × 24 in (44.6 × 61 cm)
Published 1756
Provenance unknown (R2510)

In 1730 the Corporation decided to construct a tree-lined riverside walk alongside St George's Field extending from the City walls to the mouth of the Foss, a distance of 480 yards. Sixty-six limes and sixty-four elms were planted during 1831 and 1832 to line the walk. Such was its popularity that it was extended southwards another three-quarters of a mile beyond the Foss, which was crossed by a wooden draw bridge constructed in 1738 at a cost of £110 7*s*. 0*d*. To complete the walk 340 elms were purchased from the Telford nursery in 1740. Many of the original trees had died or become dangerous by 1824, when 820 new trees, including elms, oaks, willows, maples, chestnuts, poplars, sycamores, beeches, alders, hornbeams and ashes, were purchased from Telford's successors, Thomas and James Backhouse.

The *York Courant* in 1754 commented: 'This Terrace Walk made on the banks of the River Ouse and nearly a mile long may be justly esteemed one of the most agreeable publick walks in the Kingdom for its great neatness, beautiful town and situation which is so advantageously seen in its prospect as to render it not unlike nor inferior to any of the views in Venice'.

121

John Harper

Bridge on the New Walk, 1831

Pencil
11 × 14⅞ in (27.9 × 37.9 cm)
Signed and dated 7 July 1831
Purchased, 1918 (R1654)

The original bridge over the mouth of the Foss, a wooden drawbridge, was painted a bluish colour, giving it the name, Blue Bridge, which has been retained by its four successors. It was replaced in 1768 by a handsome stone bridge. This was too low for the Foss Navigation which opened in 1794, when a wooden swivel bridge was built. By December 1857, after many reports on its unsatisfactory and dangerous condition, this was replaced by an iron lifting bridge. By a happy coincidence, during the construction of this iron bridge, the Corporation was promised two cannons captured during the siege of Sebastopol. They arrived at York station and were placed on special platforms on either side of the bridge on 5 November 1858 with great ceremony including a public dinner and speeches. The fifth and present Blue Bridge, another lifting iron bridge, was opened in May 1930. The Crimean cannons lasted until the end of 1941 when they were removed, together with other guns lining the earlier part of the New Walk, and sold as scrap metal to help the War effort.

122

Henry Cave

From the Blue Bridge, 1803

Pencil
11¼ × 17⅛ in (28.4 × 43.5 cm)
Signed and dated 1803 (on the reverse)
Provenance unknown (R3156)

St George's Field, outside the City walls, has always been an open space, although one now largely occupied by the ubiquitous motor car. In 1232 it was granted as meadow lands to the Knights Templar, an order which was suppressed in 1312. Their chapel then passed to the Crown. When the Guild of St George, one of the three great religious guilds in York, was incorporated in 1447 the chapel, by then in a dilapidated state, was given to it. Shortly after this time the field must have gained its present name. In earlier times it had been used for sports such as archery and wrestling and from 1880 was the site of York's first indoor swimming bath, now demolished. Regular fairs have been held here since their transfer from Parliament Street in 1924.

Browney Dyke, the lower reach of the Foss, just upstream of Blue Bridge, leads up to the Castle Mills, in existence since at least 1130 and until 1794 the head of navigation on this river.

123

Francis Bedford

York Castle and Clifford's Tower from the North-East, 1841

Pencil, wash, and pen and ink
5⅞ × 8⅝ in (15.1 × 21.8 cm)
Provenance unknown (R196)

However 'stately' Defoe had thought the prison early in the eighteenth century, its condition a hundred years later gave rise to some criticism from prison reformer, Joseph John Gurney. He thought the prisoners suffered from 'want of cleanliness, want of further classification, want of inspection, want of instruction, want of employment'. This, coupled with the need to apply the provisions of the Gaol Act, 1823, induced the County Magistrates to enlarge and improve the prison. Designs by G. T. Andrews and P. F. Robinson were accepted and the foundation stone was laid in 1826 followed by the erection of massive 35ft-high gritstone walls looming darkly over Tower Street. This street led to the Castle Mills Bridge, the mills themselves and the Windmill Inn, a Tudor building standing on the medieval foundations of St George's Chapel whose upper levels, in 1566, had become a stone quarry for the repair of Ouse Bridge.

124

Henry Cave

Castlegate Postern, *c.* 1800

Pencil
$7\frac{5}{8} \times 10\frac{3}{8}$ in (19.3×26.2 cm)
Purchased as part of the Evelyn Collection, 1931 (R3155)

Castlegate Postern, to the south of Clifford's Tower and outside the Castle precinct, from the fourteenth century and perhaps earlier provided a passage through the City walls for access to the Castle Mills. There does not seem to have been a roadway over the dam until 1583 when the Corporation agreed that 'a sufficient wood bridg shalbe maid with all spede beyond the Castle milns at the Cities charge for fotemen and grass men to passe.' They widened the postern in 1699 for the passage of carriages and coaches and tried, without success, to persuade the people of Castlegate to build a substantial stone bridge over the Foss. Even when such a bridge was built in 1733 wagons and other heavy vehicles were prevented from passing by a locking post at the postern while coaches and chaises were given free passage. In May 1826 the postern, which had been sold to the County Justices, was demolished to allow the enlargement of the Castle.

125

Henry Cave

Clifford's Tower, *c.* 1800

Pencil
11 × 15 in (28.1 × 38.2 cm)
Transferred from the Castle Museum, 1975
(R3154)

Some time after the withdrawal of the garrison from the Castle at the end of the seventeenth century domestic buildings started to appear round Clifford's Tower. On the south side a house has been built just outside Castlegate Postern facing St George's Field where cattle graze. As usual the builders have economized on building materials by incorporating the City walls in their structure. This house, like the Postern itself, disappeared in 1826.

126

Unidentified Artist

Clifford's Tower, *c.* 1700

Pencil, sepia and blue washes, and pen and black ink
$9\frac{1}{2} \times 16\frac{1}{4}$ in (24.3×41.5 cm), image
Presented by the Dean and Chapter of York Minster, 1948 (R1852)

Two wooden keeps preceded the stone quadrilobate structure which was built on the motte between 1245 and 1262 and reached by a wooden drawbridge over a defensive ditch. The first was destroyed in 1190 when the Jews of York, having taken refuge there from the anti-Jewish riots, set it alight in an act of mass suicide. It was rebuilt in timber afterwards. By 1360 the new stone keep was split from top to bottom in two places as a result of subsidence and required considerable repairs. Virtually redundant, it fell into decay over the next two centuries and might well have vanished altogether had not Robert Redhead, the gaoler in 1596, been stopped from demolishing it and disposing of the stone. But its defensive days were not yet over: new floors and a roof with a gun platform were built in 1642 when it was garrisoned for the King. These were destroyed on 23 April 1684 by a fire which started after a salute of seven guns, in honour of St George's Day had been fired. Although once referred to more colloquially as the 'Minced Pie', its present name of Clifford's Tower was first recorded in 1596, perhaps in recognition of an unsubstantiated claim on the part of the Earls of Clifford to be hereditary Constables of York.

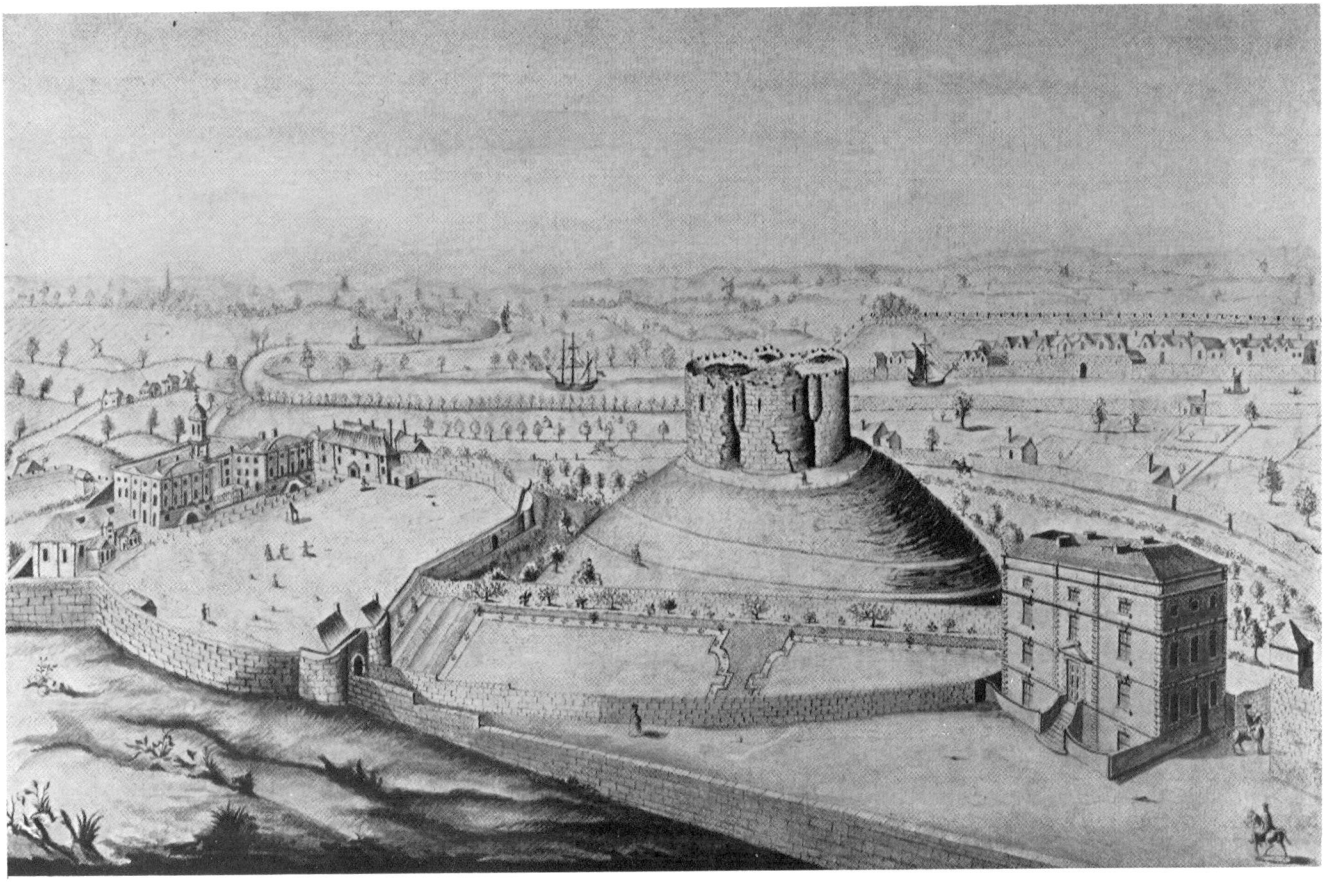

127

Unidentified Artist

Clifford's Tower and Samuel Waud's House, *c.* 1730

Pencil, pen and blue ink, and blue wash
$11\frac{3}{4} \times 18\frac{1}{2}$ in (29.9 × 47 cm), image
Presented by the Dean and Chapter of York Minster, 1948 (R1860)

After the fire in 1684 (see No. 126) Clifford's Tower remained for a few more years in the hands of the military authorities before passing, at the end of the century, to the first of a succession of private owners, Lady Suzanna Thompson. In 1699 it passed to Richard Sowray, the owner of the house on the north side of the Tower. His son, Richard, owned it until his death in 1709. Shortly after this *The Northern Atalantis; or York Spy* reported that 'the Shell of the Building upon't was an Honour and an Ornament to the City, till an old Crabbed Humorist, defaced the Mount to enlarge his Gardens'. In 1727 Samuel Waud became the owner of the house and Tower in settlement of a claim against the estate of Richard Denton, Richard Sowray's nephew and heir, who had become bankrupt. From this time the two properties stayed in the Waud family for nearly a century. In 1820, when the house was advertized for let, it was described as 'very spacious, genteelly furnished, and well suited for a family of the first respectability . . . one of the most desirable residences in York'. A wall separated the house with its splendid folly from the remainder of the Castle grounds where, from 1701, new buildings had begun to appear.

128

William Lindley

'A Perspective View of York Castle with part of the Court of Justice and Grand Jury House', *c.* 1759

Etching and wash
10¼ × 14⅞ in (26.1 × 37.8 cm)
Purchased as part of the Evelyn Collection, 1931 (R1944)

While houses were built outside the castle, the bailey, no longer needed for military purposes, was the site of a variety of public buildings needed to deal with the anti-social tendencies of some members of the civil population. Flanked by the Sessions House (1674–5) on the left and the Grand Jury House (1667–8) on the right, a new County Gaol, possibly designed by William Wakefield, was built between 1701 and 1705 and described by Defoe as 'a Prison the most stately and complete of any in the whole kingdom, if not in Europe'. This comment must have given little comfort to any of its inmates except, perhaps, the debtors for whom special accommodation was provided in the right wing along with the Governor. Although felons were by far the largest group of prisoners it was the debtors who were to give the building its name, the Debtors' Prison. The clock, with a single hand, was installed by John Terry, a York clockmaker in 1716.

129

Henry Rushbury

The Debtors' Prison, 1941

Etching and drypoint
7 × 10 in (17.9 × 25.5 cm)
Signed
Presented by the family of the late J. B. Morrell, Esq., 1964 (R1463)

In 1900 the military took over the prison, retaining it until 1929. Then after standing empty for a few years it was sold to the City Council for £8,000 in 1934. The next year the outer walls, gatehouse, governor's house and cell blocks were pulled down to make way for new municipal offices for the City. Building work began in 1938 but never progressed beyond basement level. The Female Prison was modified in 1934 to house the Kirk Collection of Bygones, the lifetime accumulation of Dr John Kirk, a Pickering general practitioner, and the nucleus of the present Castle Museum. The Debtors' Prison, used as warders' quarters after the new cell blocks were built in the 1830s, became part of the Museum in 1952. It is now joined to the Female Prison by a glass entrance lobby which has a section of the old bailey wall, with seven vaulted lavatories, as its rear wall.

130

Attributed to
Francis Bedford

The Castle Yard, *c.* 1841

Pencil, sepia wash and ink
8⅞ × 12⅛ in (22.5 × 30.7 cm)
Purchased, 1979 (R90)

The new prison was completed in 1835. Within its walls, which were entered from Tower Street by a gatehouse flanked by two drum towers, stood a circular house for the governor, from which radiated four cell blocks for the prisoners. Immured behind an inner wall, they were separated from the citizens of York and the Ridings who, watched by the governor's deer hoping for a titbit, came to the Assize Courts on lawful business. Clifford's Tower, with its motte cut back and supported by a retaining wall, still had trees within and without as a reminder of its previous life as a garden folly.

131

J. H. Lee

View in the Castle Yard, 1841

Two-toned lithograph
$8\frac{1}{2} \times 13\frac{5}{8}$ in (21.5 × 34.6 cm)), image
Signed and dated 1841
Printed by William Monkhouse, York
Purchased, 1960 (R2956)

Between 1773 and 1777 the Grand Jury House was replaced by a Court House for the assizes of the whole county, designed by John Carr (right), which, although still retaining its original façade, has been altered and extended at several dates in both the nineteenth and twentieth centuries. The building contained a room for the Grand Jury near which, from 1802, was erected, as the occasion demanded, a temporary scaffold for 'the awful sacrifice of human life to offended laws'. The present range of buildings surrounding the oval lawn, 'The Eye of the Ridings', was completed in 1802 by Peter Atkinson's addition of pavilions to the Female Prison (left), which had been erected to designs by Thomas Wilkinson and John Prince between 1780 and 1783, with a centre matching the Court House opposite. The walls of the new prison which encompassed these buildings not only retained the malefactors but prevented the governor's deer from straying into the City.

132

John Charles Varrall after William Henry Bartlett and (figures by) William Harvey

Interior of Clifford's Tower, 1828

Etching on steel
7⅞ × 6⅛ in (20.1 × 15.6 cm)
Printed by Hayward
Published by John Britton, Burton Street, London, 1 July 1828
Purchased as part of the Evelyn Collection, 1931 (R1772)

The private owners of Clifford's Tower either planted trees on the motte or failed to remove the saplings that had seeded themselves there. But whatever the cause the wooded slopes with the stonework of the ruined keep emerging from the tops of the trees made a splendid ornamental feature at the bottom of the garden. Not only did the trees spread over the motte but also into the interior, where the bosky surroundings and romantic atmosphere provided a very suitable setting for family picnics. The picnic party seen here will have reached the summit by winding paths laid out round the motte by the Waud family.

133

James Lloyd

Clifford's Tower, 1962

Pencil and bodycolour
20 × 14 in (50.9 × 35.6 cm)
Signed and dated 1962
Commissioned as the Evelyn award, 1961 (R1794)

During the period when York Castle was a prison the motte was cut back at its base and contained within a high wall. After the prison was demolished in 1935 the wall was removed and the motte was restored to its original appearance with all the trees that were causing subsidence problems removed. On the opposite side of Tower Street the last part of St George's Field to retain any vestige of its earlier use as a meadow has been laid out with formal paths and lit with electric lamps. These were mounted on columns originally installed for an earlier form of lighting — gas, which first illuminated the streets of York in 1824. Between the two World Wars many towns and cities in Britain had on display a tank brought back from the battlefields of Europe. York's tank stood in St George's Field, just inside the entrance from Tower Street and, like so much other metalwork in the City, disappeared during the next war to be recycled into more modern armaments.

134

John Piper

York from Clifford's Tower, 1951

Watercolour, bodycolour, pen and black ink, and pastel with scratching-out
22 × 27¼ in (55.9 × 69.3 cm)
Signed
Commissioned as the Evelyn Award, 1950
(R2512)

From the parapet of Clifford's Tower the panorama of the City unfolds all around. The towers and spires of its medieval churches stand out against the skyline and there is a dramatic view of the full length of the Minster, revealing the changing styles of architecture over the two centuries it took to build. Immediately below, in Castlegate, stands Fairfax House, once the home of Charles Gregory, ninth and last Viscount Fairfax, which was rescued in 1982 by the York Civic Trust from an uncertain future. From 1919 to 1965 it had beeen used with the buildings flanking it, as a dance hall and entrance lobby for a cinema, St George's Hall built behind it. Coppergate, beyond Fairfax House, was the home of one of York's sweet-manufacturing firms, M. A. Craven & Son, from 1860 to 1967, whose premises were a long factory building with a tall chimney at its west end.

135

Thomas Rowlandson

'Mary Evans hung at York August 10 1799 for Poisoning her Husband', (?)*c.* 1800

Pencil, wash, and pen and ink
$8\frac{1}{4} \times 5\frac{1}{8}$ in (21×13.1 cm)
Signed
Purchased, 1954 (R1705)

Men have no monopoly on the 'privilege' of being executed. From the first recorded execution in York in 1379 to the last in 1896 women, although in smaller numbers, have been despatched at the gallows for a variety of offences from killing husbands and illegitimate children to 'uttering forged notes', setting fire to haystacks and even 'for stealing wearing apparel of no great value'. There is no record of a Mary Evans being 'hung' in York on 10 August 1799 or at any other time, although Mary Ellah was hanged at the Tyburn on 30 March 1757 for the wilful murder of her husband by strangling. Hangings were performed in public, first at the Tyburn, and then, after 1802, at the Castle until the ghoulish practice came to an end in 1868.

136

Henry Rushbury

Debtors' Prison,
***c.* 1933– (?)1946**

Pencil, blue wash, pen and blue ink, watercolour and blue biro
$12\frac{3}{4} \times 19\frac{1}{4}$ in (32.3×49 cm), image
Signed and dated 1940 and (?)1946
Purchased, 1982 (R2210)

Since 1068, when William the Conqueror dammed the Foss to create an outer defence for his castle on the east bank of the Ouse and a fish pond to supply food for its garrison, the waters of the river have been some 12ft 6in above the level of the Ouse. To gain access to the upper reaches the Foss Navigation Company, which had obtained an Act of Parliament in 1793, needed to construct a lock, the first of eight which allowed boats to reach Sheriff Hutton. Just above the lock the previous wooden bridge was replaced by one constructed in stone with a raised round arch but its roadway was so narrow that vehicles could cross only in one direction at a time. This was widened in 1836 by adding to it on the upstream side and demolished completely by 1956, when the present dual-carriageway bridge was opened, having been made necessary by modern traffic levels.

That this drawing was started in about 1933 (the date of the related etching, No. 137) can be confirmed by the presence of the 35ft-high gritstone walls of the prison which were demolished in 1935.

137

Henry Rushbury

Debtors' Prison, 1933

Etching and drypoint
$6\frac{1}{2} \times 11\frac{1}{8}$ in (16.5×28.3 cm)
Signed and dated 1933
Purchased, 1982 (R2220)

The drawing on which this print was presumably based is No. 136. The image has been reversed from left to right in the process of making the print.

138

Francis Place

York Castle from the the Mill Bank, 1699

Pencil, grey wash and pen and ink
6 × 11½ in (15.4 × 29.1 cm)
Provenance unknown (R1569)

The Castle of York, based round the motte built by William the Conqueror on the east bank of the Ouse, was rebuilt in stone following the visit of Henry III in 1244. The bailey wall contained an area of about three acres to which access could be gained from outside by two gates, one to the north and the other, the largest and more important, to the south. This latter gate was still in use at the end of the sixteenth century but at some time in the next, probably during the Civil War when the adjacent bridge over the Foss was broken down and Castlegate Postern blocked with an earth bank to improve the defences of the City, it was permanently sealed. By the nineteenth century the gate had been almost completely demolished and the gap in the wall filled with plain masonry. The footings and drawbridge pit were exposed by excavations in 1924 and remain today to give a hint of the massive size of this vanished structure.

139

Patrick Hall

Fossgate, 1944

Watercolour and black crayon with scratching-out
12 × 14¾ in (30.5 × 37.5 cm)
Signed
Purchased, 1944 (R3160)

As the Second World War draws to a close the presence of horse-drawn vehicles crossing Foss Bridge is a reminder of the austerity and shortages of wartime which have temporarily halted the growth of motor transport. Peter Atkinson the younger designed the bridge which was built in 1811 in gritstone. The open balustrades were approved of in 1818 by historian, William Hargrove, who thought they not only improved the prospect from the bridge but also removed from small boys the temptation to run along the top at great risk to their lives! The ill-matched pair of lamps depicted here is another sign of the times. The Corporation had no funds in 1944 for such decorative trivialities but in 1975 two lamps, recovered from New Walk and painted and gilded by the Civic Trust, restored a more dignified appearance to the bridge.

140

George Nicholson

Interior of Walmgate Bar, 1827

Pencil
9⅝ × 13⅞ in (24.4 × 35.2 cm)
Dated 11 July 1827
Purchased as part of the Evelyn Collection, 1932 (R1418)

During repair work in 1584–6 a timber-framed structure was projected forward from the inner façade of Walmgate Bar supported on two stone Roman-Doric columns to allow the upper storeys to be used as a house. Perhaps its most famous occupant was John Browne, the painter and historian of York Minster, whose trade sign is displayed on the bar. John Browne's father, a joiner, and his grandfather had lived in the house, and John was born there in 1793 as John Brown, the first of eighteen children, whose presence must have made living in such a cramped space almost impossible. In 1826, when his reputation as an artist was well-established, John added the final 'e' to his surname. The Dutch-gabled building, which masks the side arch created in 1804, was pulled down before 1853.

141

Henry Cave

Walmgate Bar, *c.* 1800

Pencil
16⅞ × 15 in (27.6 × 38.3 cm)
Transferred from the Castle Museum, 1975
(R3151)

In the fourteenth century the outer defensive barbican and a façade to house a portcullis were added to the twelfth-century main arch of Walmgate Bar. Damage during the siege of York in 1644 was repaired by 1648 but, through neglect, the structure had become extremely dilapidated by the beginning of the nineteenth century. By that time a cottage had been built with its back wall against the south wall of the barbican, no doubt using stones from the bar for its other walls. Beyond the bar a narrow lane leads only to a few properties behind Lawrence Street. Foss Islands roads was not constructed until 1854 when the Corporation, having purchased the defunct Foss Navigation, drained the swamp which was the last vestige of the King's Fishpond of the Foss and laid a new road across it.

142

Thomas Shotter Boys

Lawrence Street and Walmgate Bar, *c.* 1841

Pencil and sepia ink
8⅞ × 11⅞ in (22.5 × 30.3 cm)
Purchased as part of the Evelyn Collection, 1931 (R241)

The houses on either side of broad Lawrence Street, filled with sheep and farmers' traps on a market day, frame the only surviving barbican in the country, shown here in a somewhat ruinous state with its northern wall totally collapsed and only the bases of its barbicans remaining. That it still stands today, a unique reminder of how the other three great bars of the City once looked, is due, strangely, to a railway company. The Great North of England Railway paid the Corporation £500 in 1840 for the privilege of reconstructing North Street Postern to allow horse-carts to reach the goods depot outside the walls and this money was used to pay for the repair of Walmgate Bar. The 1804 side arch was replaced in 1862 by a much larger one to improve access into the City, the problem of which, earlier in the century, had caused the loss of the three other barbicans.

143

Unidentified Artist

Heslington Hall, *c.* 1850

Pencil
9 × 11⅜ in (22.9 × 28.8 cm)
Provenance unknown (R3158)

Outside the City boundary, at Heslington, Thomas Eymes, Secretary to the Council of the North, in 1565–8 built a grand mansion, it was rumoured, for the reception of Queen Elizabeth when she visited the northern parts. If this is so he was certainly disappointed, for in the event she did not visit York. On the garden front the two square staircase towers were given inappropriate pyramidal pinnacles during an almost total rebuilding of the hall in 1852 by Yarburgh Yarburgh from Bridlington, who had inherited it that year. He had already considerably added to his former home, Sewerby Hall near Bridlington, and when Heslington Hall was complete it had 109 rooms. One wonders why an elderly bachelor needed two houses of such enormous proportions! In 1903 Walter Brierley was employed by Lord Deramore to return the hall to some semblance of its Elizabethan origins and he was responsible for the removal of the fancy pinnacles.

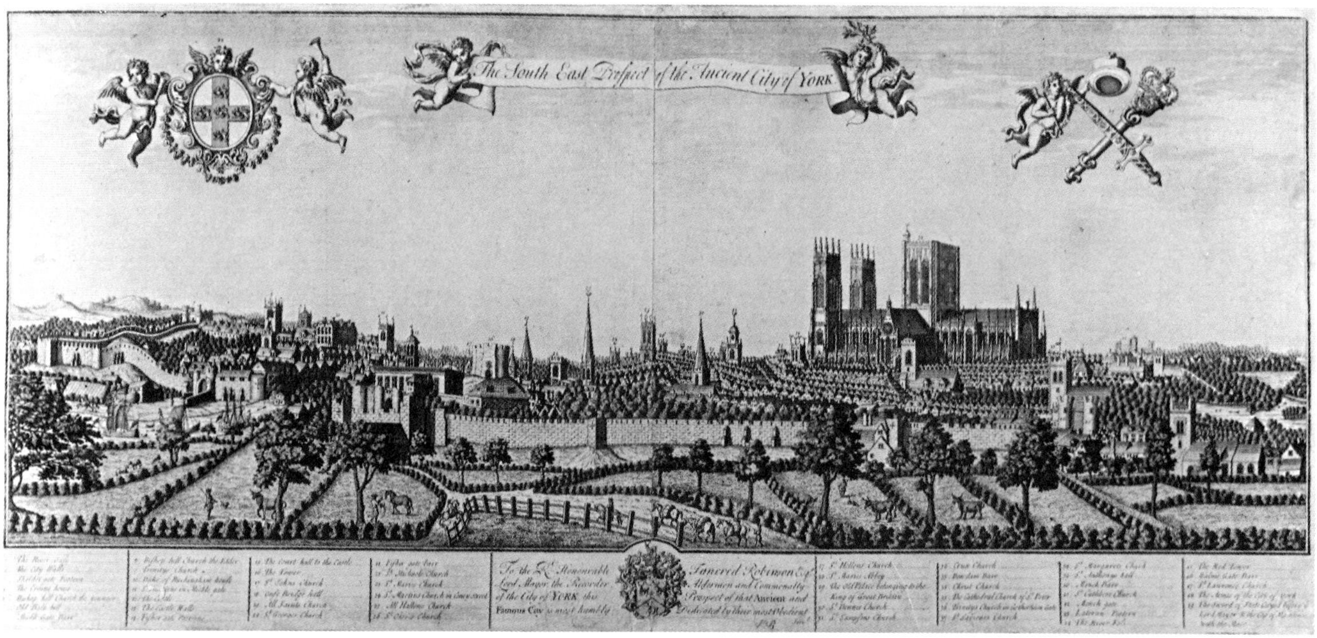

144

Edmond Barker

'The South East Prospect of the Ancient City of York', (?)1718

Etching
16⅝ × 42⅛ in (42.2 × 107 cm), image
Signed
Provenance unknown (R1803)

This panorama makes an interesting comparison with one of Place's slightly earlier views (No. 115) but the vantage-point has been moved further east, to Lamel Hill on the road from Heslington. The relativity of all the landmarks thereby changes and new ones come into view — either no longer hidden by others, like the 1697 Italianate tower of St Crux, Pavement (demolished in 1887), or newly built, like the clock tower of the Debtors' Prison near Clifford's Tower. One secular building stands prominently on the skyline amongst the churches, the great mid-sixteenth-century mansion in Bishophill between the towers of St Mary, Bishophill Senior, and St Martin, Coney Street. This was built by Thomas Fairfax, the Parliamentarian general, passed to the Duke of Buckingham in 1671 and was pulled down in the eighteenth century. The river Ouse, with at lease five ships on a short reach, sailing through the formally laid-out meadows outside the walls, is a hive of activity as might be expected of the City's major trade route.

The Topographical Collection at York

York City Art Gallery holds around 2,500 prints, drawings and watercolours of York and Yorkshire. The nucleus of this collection was bought in 1931 by public subscription from Dr William Arthur Evelyn (1860–1935) a doctor originally from Presteigne, Radnor (now Powys), who settled in York in 1891 and amassed about 1,200 images of his beloved adopted city. Other smaller collections followed by gift, and many more works were individually purchased, or presented to the Gallery. In 1950 at the instigation of the Dean of York, the Very Reverend Eric Milner-White, the Evelyn Award scheme was established. Its purpose was to bring the collection up to date by commissioning annually a living artist to paint a view of York for the sum of fifty guineas. Thirteen works were commissioned, four of which are included in this catalogue (Nos 21, 109, 133 and 134). Unfortunately it proved impossible to find sufficient artists of standing with the necessary topographical skills to undertake the annual commission and the scheme was abandoned in 1963.

Today the topographical collection ranges from the seventeenth to the twentieth centuries, concentrating on the nineteenth. It is still growing and provides an invaluable resource for the study of the changing face of York over the centuries.

Select Bibliography

Apart from standard biographical dictionaries the following are some of the works which have been useful in the compilation of the artists' biographies.

Abbey, J. R. *Scenery of Great Britain and Ireland in Aquatint and Lithography 1770–1860*, privately published, London 1952.

Abbey, J. R. *Travel in Aquatint and Lithography 1770–1860*, two volumes, privately published, London 1956–7.

Benezit, E. *Dictionnaire critique et documentaire des Peintres, Sculpteurs, Dessinateurs et Graveurs*, eight volumes, Librairie Gründ, ?Paris 1948–55.

Bryan, Michael *Dictionary of Painters and Engravers*, George Bell and Sons, London 1889.

Bullamore, Colin P. *H. B. Carter: Scarborough's Greatest Native Watercolourist*, Colin Bullamore, Scarborough 1959.

Hall, Marshall *The Artists of Northumbria* (revised edition), Marshall Hall Associates, Newcastle upon Tyne 1973.

Hardie, Martin *Water-colour Painting in Britain*, three volumes, B. T. Batsford Ltd, London 1966–8.

Hubbard, William 'George Nicholson: A neglected Yorkshire Artist', *Dalesman*, 51, November 1989, pp. 645–7.

Hughes, Janet 'The Nicholson Family', *Preview*, no. 120 xxxi, October 1978, pp. 1063–71.

Hyde, Ralph *Gilded Scenes and Shining Prospects: Panoramic Views of British Towns 1575–1900*, Yale Center for British Art, New Haven 1985.

Ingamells, John 'Joseph Halfpenny of York', *Country Life*, 3 August 1972, pp. 285–6.

Lambourne, Lionel and Hamilton, Jean *British Watercolours in the Victoria and Albert Museum*, Sotheby Parke Bernet Publications/Philip Wilson Publishers Ltd in association with the Victoria and Albert Museum, London and Totowa 1980.

Mallalieu, H. L. *The Dictionary of British Watercolour Artists up to 1920*, Antique Collectors' Club, Woodbridge 1976.

Pepper, Trevor 'A Watercolourist's Centenary: Henry Gastineau', *Country Life*, 14 October 1976, pp. 1044–5.

Peppin, Brigid, and Micklethwait, Lucy *Dictionary of British Book Illustrators: The Twentieth Century*, John Murray, London 1983.

Redgrave, Samuel *A Dictionary of Artists of the English School*, Longmans, Green and Co., London 1874.

R[ose]., A[ndrea]. *Henry Gastineau 1792–1876: Centenary Exhibition*, Birmingham Museums and Art Gallery, Birmingham 1976.

Tyler, Richard *Francis Place 1647–1728*, York City Art Gallery, York 1971.

Knowles, John Ward *York Artists* (two volumes), unpublished manuscript in York Reference Library.

Waterhouse, Ellis *The Dictionary of British 18th-Century Painters*, Antique Collectors' Club, Woodbridge 1981.

Williams, Iolo A[neurin]. *Early English Watercolours*, The Connoisseur, London 1952.

Biographies of Artists

Abbott, John White, 1763–1851. John White Abbott was an Exeter-born apothecary who was a serious amateur painter, principally of landscapes. He was the best known pupil of Francis Towne (1739/40–1816) whose drawing style he closely emulated. In June and July 1791 Abbott made his only extended tour outside the West Country, visiting York, Morpeth, Scotland, the Lake District, Liverpool, Derbyshire and Warwickshire: York City Art Gallery has all four of the known views of York made on this tour. Abbott spent his life in Devonshire, retiring from medicine to Fordland, his estate near Exeter, when he inherited money from his uncle. In 1831 he was made Deputy-Lieutenant of the county. He died in Exeter. *Nos 19, 20 and 43*

Ayrton, Michael, 1921–1975. Michael Ayrton was born in London, the son of Gerald Gould the poet (but adopted his mother's maiden name). He was educated in London, Paris, Vienna and Italy. In London he studied at Heatherley's and the St John's Wood School of Art. In Paris he shared a studio with John Minton. He was a painter of imaginative subjects and figures as well as producing portrait sculpture in bronze. He was also a theatre designer, book illustrator and writer. He particularly enjoyed depicting myths of antiquity, which were to him timeless metaphors expressing truths about the human condition. Sutherland, Moore and Tchelitchew, were the artists who influenced him most. He settled at Toppesfield in Essex.

In 1951 he was asked to produce a watercolour of York as the second work commissioned under the Evelyn Award scheme. He accepted with some trepidation and after three attempts was still unhappy with the result, which is No. 21. From letters to Hans Hess, the then Curator, in the Gallery files, it is obvious that Ayrton found both the watercolour medium and the subject 'rather unsympathetic'. Although he had 'produced a drawing with some vitality and a certain quality of design', he did not think the finished work was 'first rate Ayrton'. *No. 21*

Baker, Joseph, working 1739–died 1770. Joseph Baker was an actor, theatre-manager, painter and draughtsman. The first (probable) mention of him is as an actor in *The Twin Rivals* at the Merchant Adventurers' Hall, York. In 1744 he was employed by Mrs Thomas Keregan as manager of the new theatre in York which she opened in Blake Street on the site of the present Theatre Royal. Baker occupied the post for the next twenty-two years until succeeded by Tate Wilkinson (1739–1803). By 1748/9 Baker was living in Blake Street and was also painting scenery for the new theatre. In 1761 he was granted (under the name of Christopher Mitchell) the lease of a house in Blake Street, from 1764 for twenty-one years, on condition he made improvements. This building had previously been used as a theatre and Baker opened his own theatre there in 1765. It ruined him financially, however, and he died in 1770.

Only two pictorial images are known by Baker — perspective views of the cathedral churches of Lincoln and York, both engraved by Francis Vivares, which were first advertized in the *York Courant* in 1750. No drawing related to the Lincoln engraving is known although an oil painting signed and dated 1742 showing an identical view is now at the Usher Art Gallery, Lincoln. The original drawing for the York engraving is No. 96 in this catalogue. *No. 96*

Barker, Edmond, working 1716–1718. Edmond Barker was an engraver and print-publisher working in the early eighteenth century. His best known work is the magnificent *South-East Prospect of the Ancient City of York* probably of 1718 (No. 144). A notice advertizing the publication of this plate appeared in the *Evening Post*, 20–22 March 1718, when it was announced that the view would be completed within three months. The cost to subscribers was 2*s*. 6*d*., but those subscribing for six copies would be given a seventh free (a common sales practice at the time). Half the price was payable immediately and the other half on publication. The view, which was advertized as being as complete as possible, could be examined at a number of locations, one being at Edmond Barker's own premises in Coney Street. *Nos 90 and 144*

Bartlett, William Henry, 1809–1854. W. H. Bartlett, a prolific topographical draughtsman, was born in Kentish Town on 26 March 1809. In 1823 he was articled to John Britton for whom he executed drawings for *Cathedral Antiquities of England* and *Picturesque Antiquities of English Cities*, published between 1814 and 1835 and in 1830 respectively. He copied works by Turner, Girtin, Cotman and others and, after seven years with Britton, became a journeyman artist. In this capacity he travelled widely, visiting the Continent, Syria, Egypt, Palestine, America and Canada. During his lifetime, Bartlett illustrated twenty-eight volumes, mostly travel books, and was well-known for his thousands of steel engravings which were often copied by artists and amateurs soon after publication. Excellent at topography and landscape, Bartlett was not skilled at depicting the human form and, when figures were required, he collaborated with other artists such as William Harvey (q.v.). Bartlett's works were exhibited at the Royal Academy and at the New Society of Painters in Water-Colours between 1831 and 1833. He died at sea on 13 September 1854 whilst aboard the S.S. Egyptus bound from Malta to Marseilles. *No. 132*

Bedford, Francis, 1816–1894. Francis Bedford, watercolourist, lithographer and photographer, was born in London. He was the eldest son of the architect Francis Octavius Bedford and trained initially in his father's profession. In the early 1840s he spent about three years working with the York lithographer William Monkhouse (q.v.) at his workshop in Lendal. It was during this period, in 1843, that Bedford's two series of lithographs of York subjects, *Sketches in York* and the *Churches of York* were produced, the latter in collaboration with Monkhouse. Both were published by H. Smith of York. Bedford subsequently returned to London to work for the eminent lithographers Day & Son. He was also employed by other lithographers, contributing to several important publications during this period. Such work included one hundred lithographic plates for Owen Jones's influential *The Grammar of Ornament*, which was published in 1857.

From around 1851 Bedford became interested in photography, and from 1862 onwards was well known as a practitioner in this field. *Nos 14, 48, 85, 123 and 130*

Boddy, William James, 1832–1911. William James Boddy was a topographer and teacher of watercolour painting. He was born on 1 April 1832 in Woolwich and came to York in 1853, where he was to remain for the rest of his life. He worked initially as an assistant to the architect George Jones and then to the firm of J. B. & W. Atkinson, but he soon gave up architecture in favour of watercolour painting, advertizing himself as an 'Artist and Drawing Master' in the *Yorkshire Gazette* on 28 January 1854. As well as giving private tuition, he taught in schools, including St Peter's and St Olave's in York and Ampleforth College. His output was prolific and included many views of York, but also architectural subjects and landscapes throughout Great Britain and occasionally on the Continent. In about 1856 he published at least the first part of *Studies from Nature: A Series of Advanced Drawing Copies* (of which six were projected), containing lithographs by John Storey (q.v.) after his drawings. In 1895 he published a *Manual for Invalids Sunday by Sunday*. In 1905 thirty-four of his watercolours were reproduced in colour in an album published under the title *Historic York* with text by J. S. Fletcher. Boddy lived at a number of addresses in York and died at 2 South Parade on 12 May 1911. He was buried in Acomb, the part of York he had made his married home. His reputation was high in the early years of the century and a posthumous exhibition of his work was held at his studio in Lendal Chambers from 10 to 22 July 1911. In April and May 1912, 137 drawings and watercolours were exhibited at York City Art Gallery. The label of Wilfred H. Hurworth, gilder, picture-frame maker and fine art dealer of 79 Low Petergate, is to be found on the back of many of Boddy's framed watercolours. Hurworth acted as the artist's dealer. *No. 63*

Boys, Thomas Shotter, 1803–1874. Thomas Shotter Boys was a watercolour painter and lithographer who was born in Pentonville, Islington. He was trained as an engraver by George Cooke and around 1823 went to Paris to ply his trade. Whilst there he met Richard Parkes Bonnington with whom he became friends and whose working methods he assimilated. In Paris he began to work as a watercolourist and in lithography, the potential of which he quickly recognized. The greater part of Boys's lithographic work was executed, however, in London, after his return in 1837. There he published in 1839 *Picturesque Architecture in Paris, Ghent, Antwerp, Rouen*, in 1841 *A Series of Views of York* and in 1842 *Original Views of London as it is*. However, despite undoubted skill and recognition, his career declined after the early 1840s. By 1871 illness had made him unable to work and he died in St John's Wood, London, three years later. Boys was primarily an architectural watercolourist. His special abilities lay in accurately depicting buildings and in the handling of perspective. His drawings are skilfully composed and peopled with figures of great liveliness. At his best his touch is light and sure. *Nos 31, 70, 74, 111 and 142*

Brown, Edward, 1840–1897. Edward Brown was a lithographer and watercolourist who was born on 11 November 1840 in Easingwold, near York. He was apprenticed to Bevan and Storey, and made lithographic portraits of many local dignitaries including Francis Carr, James Lowther and William Hey. He had a great love of music and was to give up painting for teaching the violin. In 1876 he was living at Blenheim Place, Monkgate, but he died, at home, in Penley's Grove Street, York, on 23 December 1897. *Nos 78 and 84*

Brown, Henry. See under Brown, William and Henry.

Brown(e), John, 1792/3–1877. John Brown was an artist and antiquary, who was born in the house above Walmgate Bar. He originally set up in York as a house painter, but subsequently became a teacher of drawing and painting. He added the final 'e' to his name in 1826 when his reputation was well-established. Fascinated by history, architecture and archaeology, he published an illustrated pamphlet in 1827 entitled *An Attempt to ascertain the true Age of the Porch of St Margaret's Church, York*. At the same time he drew and etched a large view of the porch. His major work, however, was *The History of the Metropolitan Church of St Peter, York*, which was published from 1847 onwards in thirty-three parts at 7*s*. 6*d*. each. The whole work contained 150 illustrations drawn by Brown and etched by himself and his eldest son, William Gill Browne. The finished work represented more than twenty years' work. The detailed information contained in the drawings, especially those of the nine ceiling bosses, was invaluable for the accurate restoration of the Minster after the 1840 fire. The drawings are now at York City Art Gallery. Browne died on 9 November 1877 at the age of eighty-five at his home in Blake Street, from which address he had additionally sold books and stationery. *Nos 49, 100 and 101*

Brown, William and Henry, 1814–1877 and 1816–1870. William and Henry Brown were born in York and worked there as wood engravers. In 1836 they published eighty-three wood-engraved views of York. They subsequently settled in the Low Countries. In 1840 Henry became head of the Royal School of Engraving at the Hague in the Netherlands, and died in Antwerp. William succeeded Henry in the Hague, and died in Belgium. *No. 71*

Buck, Samuel and Nathaniel, 1696–1779 and working 1727–after 1753. The Buck brothers were extremely prolific topographical draughtsmen, engravers and publishers. They were probably both born in Richmond, Yorkshire. Samuel, the elder, embarked on his career first, working from London alone between 1711 and 1726. In 1727 Nathaniel joined him and from then until 1753 they worked in partnership, making drawings around the country in the summer and engraving the plates in the winter. Four hundred and twenty-eight views of abbeys and castles in the British Isles resulted from this labour, together with a further eighty-three panoramic views of the major cities in England and Wales. The former, originally published in parts, were reissued as Buck's *Antiquities* in 1774. Nathaniel probably died in London at some point between 1753 and 1759; Samuel carried on alone until his death in 1779.

Samuel made two sketches of York in 1719/20, both in the Warburton sketchbook, British Museum. The original drawing for the engraving of *The South View of the Ruins of St Mary's*

Abbey in York published in 1721 (No. 41) was probably also made 1719/20. Samuel's first large-scale prospect of York, the *South Prospect of the Antient City of York from the Old Baile Hill* was engraved by Vandergucht somewhere between *c*. 1720 and 1736. However, on 15 April 1745 the brothers published their best-known view of York, *The South-East Prospect of the City of York* taken from Lamel Hill (No. 117), for which three preparatory drawings exist, No. 116 being one of them. The basic composition of this engraving was adapted for other, often anonymous, engravings throughout the eighteenth century. *Nos 41, 116 and 117*

Carter, Henry Barlow, 1803–1868. Henry Barlow Carter was a watercolour artist, who specialized in topography and seascapes. Born in Scarborough, he entered the navy and had every opportunity of observing the elements whilst at sea. Between 1827 and 1830 four of his pictures were exhibited at the Royal Academy from addresses in Plymouth and London. In about 1830 Carter left the navy and went to live in Hull, where he became a master at the art school. He then returned to Scarborough, painting and teaching from his home at 16 York Place. In 1862 he moved to Torquay, where he worked for six years before his death. Carter's work was particularly influenced by the atmospheric effects achieved by artists such as J. M. W. Turner and Peter de Wint. His son, Joseph Newington Carter, was also an artist; his work is similar to that of his father in both style and subject matter. The largest collection of H. B. Carter's work is to be found in the Crescent Art Gallery, Scarborough. *No. 32*

Cattles. See Prince and Cattles.

Cave, Henry, 1779–1836. Henry Cave, a topographical artist in oil and watercolour, engraver and drawing-master, was born and died in York. He was the fourth son of William Cave (1751–1812), an engraver who taught his son printmaking. In 1810 Cave put this training to good use by publishing his series of etchings *Picturesque Buildings in York*, which are amongst the best-known views of York. A second edition was published by Rudolph Ackermann of 101 Strand, London, in 1813 and a third by Robert Sunter, bookseller and printseller at the Sign of the Bible, Stonegate, York, who had obtained the copyright. On this last edition the date 1813 was retained although Ackermann's name was removed. Cave sketched assiduously in the environs of York and further afield in Yorkshire, usually in pencil but often using wash and watercolour. He exhibited at the Royal Academy in 1814, 1822 and 1825 and published folios of sketches from nature and views of York as engravings and lithographs from 1810 until 1823. He taught at the Manor School, Peasholme Green School and other York schools. Part of his teaching involved preparing designs for young ladies' needlework. Numerous Cave-like drawings exist which are not by Cave. *Nos 5, 15, 16, 29, 55, 58, 59, 61, 69, 75, 83, 108, 110, 122, 124, 125 and 141*

Chassereau, Peter, working 1739–1750. Peter Chassereau was an architect and land surveyor, presumably of Huguenot descent, who worked in London.

On 9 August 1743 an advertisement appeared in the *York Courant* announcing the proposed publication by subscription of his plan of York the following year. The price was half a guinea and the intended print run 600 copies. Perhaps subscriptions were slow in coming in but, whatever the case, the plan of the City of York did not appear until 1750 when it was published by John Rocque (q.v.), possibly after Chassereau's death (No. 56). It was reissued with amendments in 1766, and sold by Rocque's widow in London and W. Tesseyman a bookseller in York at the much reduced price of half a crown. *No. 56*

Cuitt, George (the Younger), 1779–1854. George Cuitt, painter and etcher, was born in Richmond, Yorkshire. He was encouraged to paint by his father, George Cuitt the elder (1743–1818), who was also an artist, whilst exposure to the prints of Giovanni Battista Piranesi was a major influence on his work, and Cuitt's etchings, in their strength and vivacity, were always to be reminiscent of the Italian's style. In about 1804 Cuitt moved to Chester and taught drawing there until 1820 when he returned to Yorkshire and built a house at Masham, where he was to live for the rest of his life. From here he published his *Yorkshire Abbeys* and in 1848 his collected etchings under the title *Wanderings and Pencillings amongst the Ruins of Olden Times*. He died on 15 July 1854 at the age of seventy-five. *No. 42*

Drake, Nathan, 1727–1778. Nathan Drake was a painter in oils and watercolour, a miniaturist and a drawing-master. He was probably born in Lincoln, the son of a minor canon. His earliest known work is a north-west view of Gainsborough which was engraved by George Vertue in 1747; another drawing, of Boston, was engraved by J. S. Muller in 1751. He thus started his professional life primarily as a draughtsman. By 1752 he was living in York where he advertized in the *York Courant* on 26 December as a 'Limner and Landscape Painter' and also as a drawing-master. By 29 January 1754 Drake was advertizing the proposed publication by subscription of a print after his view of York from the New Terrace Walk, although, in the event, this was not ready until 20 July 1756 (No. 120). This print must have enjoyed considerable success but little is known of Drake's work during the next decade. He seems to have made portraits, especially in miniature, but derived his main income from teaching and cleaning pictures. In 1763 Drake married and moved from his painting room in Colliergate to Precentor's Court where he remained for the rest of his life. In 1771 he was elected a Fellow of the Society of Artists, probably on the strength of a portrait of Thomas Gent made in 1770. He also executed two portraits of Francis Drake who was probably his cousin. Nathan Drake died on 19 February 1778 and was buried in the church of St Michael-le-Belfry. He should not be confused with Nathaniel Drake, a London artist working at the same time, with whom Nathan Drake was acquainted. *No. 120*

Farington, Joseph, 1747–1821. Joseph Farington was a landscape painter and topographical draughtsman who was born in Leigh, Manchester, on 21 November 1747. He went to London in 1763 and became a pupil of Richard Wilson, and then one of the first pupils at the Royal Academy Schools. While undertaking extensive sketching tours (mainly in the North), Farington developed two main specialities — river landscapes, and mountainous subjects. In 1781 he settled in London and soon became an enormously influential figure in the Royal Academy. He is best-known not for his pictures or drawings, but for the diaries he wrote from 1793 until 1821. These give an unrivalled account of the life of the London art world at the turn of the century and provide essential source material for the art historian. Farington died in Didsbury, Manchester, on 30 December 1821.

Ouse Bridge was a very popular Yorkshire subject for draughtsmen working in the Picturesque style in the late eighteenth century. The pen and wash drawing No. 65 is a particularly large and ambitious composition and is regarded as amongst the finest Farington produced. It is believed to be a preparatory drawing for the oil painting of the same subject, first exhibited in 1784 and now hanging at the Merchant Adventurers' Hall in York. As usual in Farington's art, the drawing is more successful than the finished oil, which lacks the vitality and accuracy of the former. An almost identical (although unsigned and less firmly-executed) version of the drawing is in the City Museum and Art Gallery, Birmingham. *No. 65*

Finden, Edward Francis, *c.* 1792–1857. Edward Finden was a London-born engraver who worked closely with his elder brother William (1787–1852) and with pupils and assistants. He is reputed not to have produced any important work on his own. Joint publications include *The Gallery of British Art* and *The Beauties of Thomas Moore*. Finden died in London after a long illness. *No. 95*

Findley, A. H., working *c.* 1900. A. H. Findley was presumably a British artist, and probably an amateur, who worked at the turn of the nineteenth century. The watercolour No. 77 is the only example of this artist's work in the collection and indeed the only example known. No other information has come to light. *No. 77*

Flanders, Dennis, born 1915. Dennis Flanders is a prolific topographical artist working in the line and wash tradition. He was born on 2 July 1915 and was educated at the Merchant Taylors' School and the Regent Street Polytechnic. He subsequently studied at St Martin's School of Art and the Central School of Arts and Crafts. From 1938 he began to produce topographical drawings for magazines and newspapers and worked as a 'Special Artist' to the *Illustrated London News* between 1956 and 1964. He has exhibited in one-man and group shows in London and elsewhere, predominantly in the United Kingdom. In 1970 he was made a member of the Royal Society of British Artists and in 1976 a full member of the Royal Society of Painters in Water-Colours. Many of his drawings have been published as prints, and others illustrate books. In 1984 his own book *Britannia* was published. Flanders continues to paint and exhibit today. *No. 87*

Foster, Myles Birket, 1825–1899. Myles Birket Foster, a gifted and prolific watercolour painter of finely-detailed genre scenes, was born at North Shields but came to London at the age of five. He was educated at Quaker Schools in Tottenham and Hitchin and was then apprenticed to the leading wood engraver Peter Landells, for whom he then worked as a magazine illustrator. In 1846 he left Landells and set up independently. In the following years he presumably taught himself watercolour painting for, by 1859, he was making his living in this medium, having abandoned wood engraving altogether. In 1862 he was elected a full member of the Old Water-Colour Society with which he was to be an assiduous exhibitor. In 1852, 1853 and 1861 Birket Foster travelled on the Continent, chiefly on the Rhine, making numerous colour studies and pencil notes. In 1863 he built a house at Witley, near Godalming in Surrey, and from that time based many genre scenes on the Surrey countryside. Birket Foster remained at Witley until ill health forced him to move to Weybridge in 1893.

Birket Foster's work enjoyed enormous popularity in his day and, as part of the general reinstatement of Victorian art, has regained much of that popularity today. *No. 35*

Gastineau, Henry, 1791/2–1876. Henry Gastineau was a prolific Picturesque topographer in watercolour. He was born in London of Huguenot origins and was apprenticed to an engraver before studying oil painting at the Royal Academy Schools. He exhibited at the Royal Academy from 1812, but it was the Old Water-Colour Society (formed in 1804) which was of particular importance for him, as the Royal Academy would accept only painters in oil at this time. He became a full member of the Society in 1823, and from 1818 until 1875 contributed an average of twenty-five works twice-yearly, becoming its staunchest supporter. In common with many fellow topographical artists he travelled widely in the British Isles, and in Switzerland and Italy from 1829 onwards, sometimes with his friend J. M. W. Turner, whose work influenced his style. Gastineau was particularly attracted to mountain scenery on these sketching tours and from 1833 produced many drawings for topographical publications. A large collection of his work is at Birmingham Museum and Art Gallery. Gastineau's work is technically excellent but seldom impressive. No. 64 is a rare exception, and is furthermore unusual in being a moonlit view of York. *No. 64*

Griffith, Moses, 1747–1819. Moses Griffith, born in Caernarvonshire, was a topographical draughtsman. He came from a poor background and was self-taught as an artist. From 1769 he was employed by Thomas Pennant (1726–1798), an antiquary and natural historian, as a drawing man-servant. With Pennant he undertook several tours of the British Isles between 1769 and 1783, making large numbers of drawings intended to illustrate Pennant's writings. These tours included Yorkshire in 1773 and 1777. On the latter tour made during May and June, York was visited: four watercolours of the City which resulted are now at York City Art Gallery: *Micklegate Bar* (No. 17), the *Multangular Tower* (No. 46), '*St Sepulcre's Abbey*' (No. 107) and *St Helen's Church*. Griffith's drawings were little known until 1938 when Pennant's collection was sold at Christie's. *Nos 17, 46 and 107*

Grignion, Charles, 1716–1810. Charles Grignion was an important engraver, who was apparently born in Covent Garden. He studied in Paris and subsequently became a member of the St Martin's Lane Academy in London. He worked for many of the best-known eighteenth-century British artists, including William Hogarth (1697–1764) and Hubert Gravelot (1699–1773). In 1755 he was amongst the artists chosen to sit on a committee to establish what was to be the Royal Academy. Sadly his style went out of fashion and he died in poverty in Kentish Town on 1 November 1810; he was buried there in the churchyard of St John the Baptist. *No. 120*

Halfpenny, Joseph, 1748–1811. Joseph Halfpenny was a drawing-master, watercolourist and etcher who was born in Bishopthorpe, a village just outside York, on 9 October 1748. His father was gardener to the Archbishop of York, and in 1762 Halfpenny was apprenticed to Thomas Chapman, a York house painter. At the end of the statutory seven-year period, he set up on his own as a house, coach and sign painter in Stonegate, opposite the Star Inn, and was soon advertizing in the *York Courant* for an apprentice. During the 1770s he etched portraits and became involved with the York Theatre Royal, painting scenery for at least two productions held there. By 1780 Halfpenny had begun to make drawings and by 1787 was sufficiently proficient to act as drawing-master. In 1791 and 1792 he made tours of the Yorkshire Dales and the Lakes respectively. Generally, however, his drawings are of York. Today Halfpenny is best known for his two publications *Gothic Ornaments in the Cathedral Church of York*, published in twenty instalments between 1795 and 1800, and *Fragmenta Vetusta, or the Remains of ancient Buildings in York*, published in 1807. Additionally between 1816 and 1817 a set of etchings of *Yorkshire Churches* was published posthumously. Halfpenny had purchased a house in Gillygate which was to be his home until his death in 1811. *Nos 62 and 93*

Hall, William Patrick, born 1906. Patrick Hall was born in York on 16 December 1906. He was educated at St Peter's School and afterwards studied at the York School of Art. He began his career working mainly in lithography and etching but later devoted himself entirely to watercolour and bodycolour. He clearly knew Henry Rushbury (q.v.) well, and may have been influenced by his style: the two artists' working methods are very similar and existing drawings indicate that they worked side by side on the same spot, on several occasions. Hall has had his work shown regularly at the Royal Academy from 1928 onwards and at numerous other locations in York and elsewhere, taking part in both one-man and group exhibitions. His output consists predominantly of architectural and landscape subjects recorded both at home and abroad. He moved to London in 1946, where he became secretary of the Chelsea Arts Club. He now lives just outside Dover in Kent. *Nos 82 and 139*

Harper, John, 1809–42. John Harper was born near Blackburn, in Lancashire. An architect, he began his career under Benjamin and Philip Wyatt in London, helping them with plans for Apsley and York Houses. From London he moved to York to set up his own practice and received commissions from a number of influential patrons. At York he re-designed the façade of the Theatre Royal, giving it a pseudo-Elizabethan gable above and arcaded entrance below (demolished when the present Victorian Gothic front was erected), besides making extensive alterations and improvements to the interior. Another noteworthy commission was the building which is now St Peter's School in Clifton. He was a great friend of the artist William Etty (1787–1849), with whom he shared a keen enthusiasm to preserve the ancient buildings of York and to promote the cause of art. With his brother Edward, he largely organized an exhibition of work by living artists held in York in 1836. A prolific sketcher of landscape and architectural subjects, he was praised by Etty for his 'elegant execution and correct detail'. In 1842 Harper set out on a tour of the Continent from which numerous sketches resulted. Whilst in Rome he caught malarial fever and he died shortly afterwards at Naples when he was only thirty-three. *Nos 2, 52, 53 and 121*

Harvey, William, 1796–1866. William Harvey, a wood engraver and draughtsman, was born on 13 July 1796 in Newcastle upon Tyne. He was apprenticed to the well-known wood engraver Thomas Bewick (1753–1823) moving to London in 1817 to work for B. R. Haydon (1786–1846). In 1824 he stopped wood engraving and thereafter worked entirely as a draughtsman. He specialized in drawing figures for topographical scenes by other artists. He died on 13 January 1866 in Richmond, Surrey. *No. 132*

Haynes, John, working 1728–1755. John Haynes was a schoolmaster and engraver on leather and metal before he established himself as a topographical artist around 1730. He worked mostly in York but later in London. He received his Freedom of York as a saddler in 1728 and by 1730 was illustrating Thomas Gent's *York*. He provided a number of plates for Francis Drake's *Eboracum* of 1736 and advertized in the *York Courant* on 9 September 1740 as printing on leather, printing from copper plates, land surveying, taking perspective views of gentlemen's seats and engraving coats of arms on plate, all from an address in the Minster Yard, York. By 1751 he had moved to London where he was last recorded in 1755.

No. 92 is probably, but not certainly, the original drawing by John Haynes from which an engraving of 1741 was taken. The letterpress to the engraving gives the date of Haynes's drawing as 1735. An earlier engraving of the subject by J. Harris after Haynes was published in Francis Drake's history of York, *Eboracum*. Minor differences are visible between the drawing and both engravings, notably concerning the figures and the diamond pattern of the floor. *No. 92*

Hogarth, Arthur Paul, born 1917. Paul Hogarth, painter, draughtsman and illustrator, was born on 4 October 1917 at Kendal now in Cumbria, the son of a master butcher and farmer. Between 1933 and 1936, he studied at Manchester College of Art, going on to St Martin's School of Art, London, where he studied between 1938 and 1940. From 1950 to 1982 he held a variety of lecturing posts at London art colleges and elsewhere. In 1954 he visited China and ever since has worked as an artist–reporter and social commentator as well as an illustrator. His output also includes architectural drawing and both text and illustrations for guide books on American cities. During the 1950s and 1960s he usually worked in charcoal or soft pencil on good quality paper, but subsequently became interested in colour and lithography. Hogarth's output is predominantly topographical, but blended with caricature. He has exhibited in London, the provinces and abroad, and his work is represented in several public collections. He lived in London, and now lives in Majorca. *No. 109*

Hunter, J. A., *c.* 1768–1798. J. A. Hunter was almost certainly John Alexander Hunter, the eldest son of Dr Alexander Hunter (1733–1809), whose garden is shown in the foreground of No. 97. Presumably a gifted amateur painter, little is known about this artist except that he married Henrietta Saul of Lancaster in 1796 and died at the early age of thirty in March 1798. His father is better documented, being an Edinburgh-born doctor of medicine with extensive literary interests and with several publications to his name. He came to York in 1763 and founded the York Lunatic Asylum in Bootham Park. He had two sons and one daughter who all sadly died during his lifetime. He himself died on 17 May 1809 in Petergate. A memorial to the Hunter family can be found in the church of St Michael-le-Belfry. *No. 97*

Kip, John, *c.* 1652–1722. Jan or John Kip, the engraver, was born in Amsterdam but came to England soon after the Revolution. He engraved views of the royal palaces and other mansions mostly after drawings by Leonard Knyff for *Britannia Illustrata*, 1714, contributed views to Strype's *Stowe's Survey*, 1720, and engraved Gloucestershire mansions for Atkyn's history of Gloucestershire. His output also included engraved portraits, birds and other subjects. He died in Westminster when nearly seventy years of age. *No. 91*

Lee, J. H., active 1841. Nothing is recorded about J. H. Lee. However, on the evidence of No. 131, dated 1841, it would appear that he was a draughtsman and lithographer working in a style not dissimilar to that of Francis Bedford (q.v.). *No. 131*

Lindley, William, *c.* 1739–1818. William Lindley (sometimes spelt Linley) was probably the first assistant of the architect John Carr of York (1723–1803), with whom he worked for twenty years until 1773. Four engravings of Carr buildings taken from drawings by Lindley are at York City Art Gallery: *Kirby Hall*, *A View of the Grand Stand and Part of the Horse Course on Knavesmire near York* (No. 11), *A Perspective View of the Inside of the Grand Assembly Room in Blake Street, York* (No. 72), and *A Perspective View of York Castle with Part of the Court of Justice and Grand Jury House* (No. 128). The last three were also engraved by Lindley. In 1773 he set up as an architect on his own account. In 1774 the corporation of Doncaster asked Lindley to make a plan for a playhouse, which was built in 1775. In 1783 he became a freeman of Doncaster and by 1790 had moved there. In 1792 he entered partnership with Charles Watson and later, in *c.* 1810, with John Woodhead. He died in Doncaster on 28 February 1818 at the age of seventy-nine. Lindley was a competent but unadventurous architect working in the Carr style. *Nos 11, 72 and 128*

Lloyd, James, 1905–1974. James Lloyd, a self-taught 'naive' painter, was born in Alsager, Cheshire, on 12 October 1905, the son of a policeman who had taken up farming. Up to the age of nineteen he assisted on the farm and then, following his father's footsteps, joined the police force. Lloyd subsequently worked as a gasworks stoker, bus conductor, builder's labourer and lamp-lighter, until joining the Coldstream Guards. On demobilization, he married and settled briefly as a farm worker in Shropshire. In 1950 he and his family moved to Yorkshire, settling in 1953 at Skirpenbeck near York, where Lloyd found employment as a cowman. By this time he had begun to paint seriously and from then on he was to paint an average of one picture per week in his spare time. In 1965 Lloyd was able to devote himself solely to painting and he received wide public acclaim with a series of exhibitions at the Portal Gallery, London, in 1964, 1966, 1968 and 1971, being described by L. S. Lowry in 1968 as 'the most important British naive painter of today'. He died at the Purey Cust Nursing Home, York, on 10 March 1974.

No. 133, commissioned as the Evelyn Award in 1961, was the first work by Lloyd to enter a public collection. It is painted in a multitude of dots, a technique he derived from copying the grainy texture of half-tone illustrations in newspapers. *No. 133*

Lodge, William, 1649–1689. William Lodge, an amateur artist and engraver, was born on 4 July 1649 into a prosperous Leeds merchant family. After studying at Jesus College, Cambridge, and Lincoln's Inn, he travelled in France and Italy in 1670 and 1671, initially accompanying Lord Fauconberg's embassy to Venice. Back in England in 1671 he became a member of the York Virtuosi, a group which met to discuss a wide range of topics from the sciences to the arts. It included Henry Gyles, Dr Martin Lister, Francis Place (q.v.), and Ralph Thoresby, and Gyles was host for the meetings at his home in Micklegate (probably the present number 68). In 1678 Lodge accompanied Francis Place on a walking tour of 'seven thousand miles in seaven weekes' through South Wales. He worked closely with Place on several drawings and engravings of York and their work is not always easy to tell apart. Lodge was buried at Harewood on 27 August 1689. *Nos 1 and 40*

Mackenzie, Frederick, 1787–1854. Frederick Mackenzie was an architectural and topographical draughtsman, a pupil of John Adey Repton (1775–1860), the architect son of Humphrey Repton, famous as a landscape-gardener. Originally trained as an architect, Mackenzie supplied architectural and topographical drawings to some of the best-known publishers and engravers of his time, including Britton, Ackermann, the Havells, and the Le Keuxs. In 1823 he became a member of the Old Water-Colour Society and acted as its treasurer from 1831 until his death. During the 1830s and 1840s he worked on a number of important publications, including *Memorials of Oxford*, 1837, and *Memorials of Cambridge*, 1841–2. Towards the end of his life his skills were less in demand owing to the introduction of photography. His style, which can be described as neat, accurate and attractive, is reminiscent of that of Augustus Charles Pugin (1762–1832), with whom he sometimes worked. His published works also included *Etchings of Landscapes for the Use of Students*, 1812, and *Illustrations of the principal Antiquities of Oxfordshire*, 1823. *Nos 104, 105 and 106*

Monkhouse, William, 1813–1896. William Monkhouse came to York at the age of six when his father was appointed a gardener to the Dean of York. He enjoyed drawing from an early age and it was suggested he should try lithography, which had been introduced into York by a bookseller in Pavement called Watson. When Watson's business began to decline, Monkhouse persuaded his father to buy him a lithographic press. Accordingly he went to London, bought one from Haag & Day, and set up business in York. He worked closely with Francis Bedford (q.v.) and the business flourished. After Bedford's departure to London, Monkhouse worked with Smith, J. Stead and Bevan, producing — amongst other work — some excellent portraits. Always an innovator, he is credited as being the first lithographer working in York to introduce colour. In 1864, through Bedford's influence, Monkhouse transferred his business to his two chief assistants, Newbald and Stead, and joined Pumphrey as a professional photographer in the city. With Pumphrey and Rowntree he brought about the *Yorkshire Fine Art and Industrial Exhibitions* in York. He died at the age of eighty-four. *Nos 18, 26, 28, 48, 51, 78, 103*

Monomy, Peter, 1681–1749. Peter Monomy was a prolific marine painter, who was born into a family from Guernsey settled in London. His name appears as the artist on a print of the *South West View of York* (No. 118) published in Francis Drake's *Eboracum* of 1736. It is, however, by no means certain that Monomy visited York to make the drawing on which the print was based: it was frequent practice at the time for artists to base drawings or paintings on sketches by other hands, and Drake may well have sent Monomy a rough sketch of this scene to work up. This print, which was folded for inclusion in *Eboracum*, would presumably also have been sold separately. *No. 118*

Moore, William (the Younger), 1817–1909. William Moore, a landscape painter and topographer, was the fourth son of the portrait painter William Moore the elder (1790–1851). He was born at Birmingham in 1817 into an exceptionally artistic family, four of his twelve siblings also being painters. He was taught drawing first by his father and subsequently by H. B. Carter (q.v.) and T. M. Richardson the younger of Newcastle. As a young man, Moore drew chiefly in pencil and published lithographs of Westminster Abbey, Halifax Parish Church, and Old Malton Priory Church. However, from about 1838 he began to use watercolour and went on sketching tours in the British Isles or in Switzerland during the summer, whilst making his living by teaching during the rest of the year. A prolific artist and competent draughtsman, Moore was hindered by defective sight brought about by overstrain in youth. He exhibited regularly at the Dudley Gallery and at the (Royal) Institute of Painters in Water-Colours, and lived mainly in Yorkshire where his father had moved the family from Birmingham. A large number of his and his family's works are at York City Art Gallery. *Nos 27 and 47*

Munn, Paul Sandby, 1773–1845. Paul Sandby Munn, a watercolour painter predominantly of topography, was born in Greenwich, the son of a carriage decorator and landscape painter. The artist Paul Sandby (1725–1809), a family friend, was godfather to young Munn and probably taught him draughtsmanship. By 1799 Munn was exhibiting landscapes at the Royal Academy and between 1802 and 1813 eight of his drawings were used by the publisher John Britton in the *Beauties of England and Wales*. In 1799 he became a member of the Sketching Club (founded by Girtin) and later secretary. John Sell Cotman (1782–1842) was amongst the members and the two artists became friends, although Cotman does not seem to have influenced Munn's style. Between 1802 and 1804 Cotman spent a great deal of time helping Munn to produce drawings for young ladies to use for copying. These included the results of sketching tours they made together in Wales (1802) and Yorkshire (1803), and were sold in the stationery and print shop run by Munn's brothers. Munn was elected an associate of the Old Water-Colour Society in 1805 and exhibited forty works between then and 1815 when he left, never having been made a full member. He seems to have settled at Hastings as a drawing-master but after 1832 was mainly preoccupied with music. Munn's work may be described as sound but pedestrian. *No. 98*

Nash, Frederick, 1782–1856. Frederick Nash, an architectural draughtsman, watercolourist and teacher, was born in Lambeth, the son of a builder. He was determined to be an artist and his family placed him with Thomas Malton (1748–1804), training with whom determined the direction his art would take. After attending the Royal Academy Schools, he began his career as an architectural draughtsman, working mainly for engravers but also for architects such as Sir Richard Smith. Around 1807 he was appointed architectural draughtsman to the Society of Antiquaries for whom he worked for many years. One of his most important commissions was a series of drawings of the ruins of St Mary's Abbey, York, which he lithographed himself and brought out in 1829. He was also elected a member of the Old Water-Colour Society. He visited Durham, Switzerland, and Paris, Normandy, and the Loire: a number of important publications resulted from these travels. In 1834 he moved from London to Brighton, which remained his home for the rest of his life. From this period Sussex and Windsor Castle are the most common of his English subjects, although he continued to travel, visiting the Rhine and the Moselle in 1838 and the Lake District in 1841. Throughout his career he taught drawing and often worked up his pupils' sketches. He died on 5 December 1856 in Brighton. *No. 54*

Nattes, John Claude, c. 1765–after 1822. John Claude Nattes, a draughtsman, drawing-master, mounter of drawings and (possibly) dealer, was born in England of Irish parents. The pupil of the Irishman Hugh Primrose Dean, he exhibited Italian scenes between 1781 and 1784, and travelled in Scotland between 1797 and 1800 making views for J. Stoddart's *Remarks on Scotland*. In 1804 he published *Scotia Depicta* and became one of the founders of the Old Water-Colour Society. However, in 1807 he was expelled for exhibiting the works of others in his name. He was a member of the Sketching Society. Nattes was a diligent topographical draughtsman whose views were engraved in a number of publications. He usually used bodycolour in his coloured drawings, and made a vast number of drawings in pen and ink, sometimes with India ink wash. These have a coarse boldness of touch which is characteristic but not often attractive. Between 1820 and 1822 he was travelling in Italy and the South of France. He died in South Molton Street, London. *No. 13*

Nicholson, George (the Younger), 1787–1878. George Nicholson was baptized at Malton on 3 November 1787. A prolific topographical artist who painted in oils and watercolour, he also made lithographs and etchings. Most of his surviving output is in the form of etchings, sketchbooks and drawings. He came from an artistic family: his cousins Marianne and Sophia Nicholson were artists, but their father and his uncle Francis Nicholson is the best known of the family, being very successful in his day. George Nicholson's career remained provincial, though he probably worked with his uncle early in life. His surviving sketchbooks and drawings record picturesque scenes often ignored by other artists, and the accuracy of his work makes it a valuable source of information for today's architectural historian. He sketched extensively in Yorkshire from 1806 to 1830, but drawings also exist from tours in Bedfordshire, the Lakes, Lancashire, Lincolnshire, Northumberland, Nottinghamshire, London and the Home Counties, and France and Italy. He published a folio entitled *Six Etchings of ancient Churches in the North Riding of Yorkshire*, Malton, 1825, and made two sets of etchings of York churches in 1825 and 1827 which do not appear to have been published. He exhibited at the Royal Academy and the British Institution in 1831 and 1832. He died at the age of ninety-one at Filey and was buried in Old Malton churchyard. *Nos 24, 25, 44, 45, 89 and 140*

Nutting, Joseph, c. 1660–1722. Joseph Nutting was an engraver who practised in London. His output mainly comprised book illustrations, which were often portraits. *No. 90*

Payne, William, c. 1760–c. 1830. William Payne, watercolourist and drawing-master, was possibly born and brought up in Plymouth. He certainly moved from there to London in 1790, becoming one of the most successful and fashionable drawing-masters of his day. His success as a teacher largely depended upon his ability to provide drawings which were easily copied. No. 113 is perhaps based on a plate in a drawing manual, several of which

Payne is known to have produced. If so, its precise source has not yet been identified. Payne's popularity waned as his conventions became overworked. One enduring claim to fame, however, was his development of the pigment 'Payne's Grey' which is still available today. *No. 113*

Piper, John, born 1903. John Piper was born on 13 December 1903 at Epsom in Surrey. He was educated at Epsom College, Richmond School of Art and at the Royal College of Art. He had begun to study art at the age of twenty-three, and has since then made full use of every medium available to the artist. His work includes stained glass, stage sets, pottery, tapestries and textiles, as well as painting, drawing and prints, and also writing. In youth he showed a keen interest in architecture, studying the stained glass and making drawings of Surrey churches, and, despite experimenting with abstraction in the 1930s and other artistic involvements, Piper has remained a devoted and inspired interpreter of buildings and places. His work is represented in major collections throughout the world, and he is indeed one of the country's best-known living artists.

John Piper was the first artist commissioned to make a contemporary topographical view of York under the Evelyn Award scheme, and No. 134 is perhaps the outstanding achievement of that scheme. Piper's painterly and architectural interests were ideally suited to the commission. *York from Clifford's Tower* exemplifies Piper's vigorous and emotive style: an exciting and dramatic work of art, it is nevertheless clearly and recognizably based on the City of York. *No. 134*

Place, Francis, 1647–1728. Francis Place was an amateur topographer, watercolourist, engraver and potter who was born into a landed family in Dinsdale, County Durham. In 1665 he went to London to study law and there met Wenceslaus Hollar (1607–1677) who introduced him to topographical drawing and etching. Place left London during the Plague of 1666 but returned to work with Hollar and became one of the earliest practitioners of mezzotint engraving. During the 1670s he travelled in Britain and the Netherlands and published sets of landscape etchings. In about 1675, he moved to York, where he had family connections. Here, he soon became the central figure amongst the York Virtuosi. During the 1680s he continued to tour Britain and at this time experimented with stoneware pottery. From 1692 he lived at the King's Manor, making journeys to Ireland, Wales, and throughout northern England until the end of his life, sometimes with William Lodge (q.v.) who shared his passion for drawing, etching and fishing. He died at the King's Manor on 21 September 1728 and is buried at St Olave's Church. Aspects of Place's work, such as his wash drawings of pure landscape without architectural features of any kind, make him a forerunner of the English watercolour school. *Nos 57, 91, 115 and 119*

Prince and Cattles, working 1805. Prince and Cattles were print-publishers under whose imprint a set of engraved views of the four York bars appeared in 1805. One or both had perhaps been involved in designing or engraving the plates. These prints are naive in style but have charm. *Nos 3 and 30*

Prout, John Skinner, 1806–1876. John Skinner Prout, a landscape and architectural painter was born in Plymouth. His style is similar to that of his more famous uncle, Samuel Prout (1783–1852), but it is thought he was largely self-taught. He painted in watercolour and some of his drawings were published as lithographs in the following: *Antiquities of Chester*, 1838, *Castles and Abbeys of Monmouthshire*, 1838, *Antiquities of York*, 1840, and *Sydney Illustrated*, 1842–4. He became a member of the New Water-Colour Society in 1838, but lost his membership as he failed to exhibit during a lengthy visit to Australia. He was re-elected to the Society as an associate in 1849 and became a full member again in 1862. He travelled in Britain and in France as well as Australia and lived in Bristol for many years. He died in London. *Nos 4 and 79*

Richardson, William, working c. 1842–c. 1877. William Richardson was the son of a York cabinet-maker at 45 Stonegate. He was articled to the York architect George Townsend Andrews and specialized in architectural drawings. He is best known for his *Monasteries of Yorkshire*, a series of lithographs after his drawings executed by George Hawkins, which was published in 1843 by Robert Sunter of 23 Stonegate, York, with historical descriptions by the Revd Edward Churton. Richardson exhibited at the Royal Academy and elsewhere from 1842 to 1877. *Nos 38, 39 and 80*

Ridsdale Tate, Edwin, 1862–1922. Edwin Ridsdale Tate was an architect, amateur artist, antiquarian and archaeologist. Brought up in York, he was educated at the Model School in Lord Mayor's Walk, St John's College and Scarborough College. He subsequently worked for Gould and Fisher, a firm of architects in Castlegate, whilst also studying at the York School of Art. Around 1885 he went to work as an architect in London, where he specialized in the restoration of ancient buildings; Bamborough Castle in Yorkshire was one of his most important commissions. After working on his own in London and Carlisle he returned to settle in York. Here he specialized in ecclesiastical work including the restoration of the fire-damaged Selby Abbey and the tower of St Mary Bishophill Junior. He also did design work for guide books such as the cover of the catalogue to the *Exhibition of Old York Views & Worthies*, 1905. He designed the street decorations for the York Pageant of 1909.

When not earning his living, sketching and photography took up much of his time. Archaeology was a major interest and, together with Walter Harvey Brook, Ridsdale Tate was responsible for important excavation work at St Mary's Abbey. The combination of this interest and a facility with pencil and pen and ink enabled him to produce some fascinating (if not totally accurate) reconstructions of how York looked in earlier times. His publications include *Quaint & Historic York*, 1906. He died on 12 June 1922 at his home, 20 Priory Street, in York. *Nos 33, 99 and 114*

Rocque, John, c. 1704–1762. John Rocque, a Huguenot who settled in England, was a mapmaker of note working from various addresses in London. He began his career as a landscape gardener but by 1743 had changed professions to become a cartographer. Work over the next few years culminated in the production of his large-scale county maps. Until 1750 he was also employed making plans of the estates of the nobility. This work encouraged him to develop a realistic style of engraving to represent different types of cultivated land. Another idiosyncratic development was his indication of the steepness of hills by shading. Around 1750 Rocque must have been developing his publishing business, for in 1753 he issued a list which offered around seventy publications and numerous maps. He presumably maintained contact with

France and probably sold his maps there: many of his publications have French sub-titles and others, such as the plan of the City of York (No. 56), have their titles entirely in French.

Sadly, despite great industry and undoubted skill in his chosen profession, Rocque died in poverty. *No. 56*

Rogers, J., working 1829. J. Rogers was a steel engraver working around 1829. In that year he engraved a plate of the '*Manor Palace*' after a drawing by Nathaniel Whittock for the London publisher I. T. Hinton. Nothing further is known about this engraver. *No. 50*

Rowlandson, Thomas, 1756–1827. Thomas Rowlandson, the brilliant draughtsman and caricaturist, was born in London. He entered the Royal Academy Schools in 1772 and visited Paris, where he had relatives, probably in 1774. In common with many artists of his day, he made a number of trips abroad and around the British Isles, probably visiting York in about 1800. Of the drawings of York now at York City Art Gallery, one is dated 1800 (No. 7), another 1801 (No. 37) and yet another 1820 (No. 6). His dates however are notoriously unreliable, as in later years he is known to have affixed dates casually. He must have visited York at some time, however, as No. 36 is clearly a sketchbook drawing made on the spot rather than a drawing worked up in the studio. From 1798 onwards much of Rowlandson's work was for the publisher Rudolph Ackermann. This included most notably *The Microcosm of London* (in association with A. C. Pugin), and the three *Tours of Dr Syntax*, which proved enormously popular. He revisited France in 1814 and went to Italy in about 1820, and was working until almost the end of his life. He died in London.

Rowlandson was not an accurate topographical draughtsman, for exactitude was not his aim. He simply put in enough topographical detail to suggest a particular geographical location, if that was required. For instance, the Minster Towers locate the racecourse in No. 12 as being at York, while the gateway similarly locates the busy street in No. 6; otherwise the topographical details in these two scenes are not correct.

There are many fake Rowlandsons and Rowlandson signatures. The demand for this drawings was enormous. One of his devices for speeding up production was to make a drawing in printing ink. This could then be covered by a damp piece of paper and run through a printing press resulting in an offset image which could quickly be retouched and strengthened to produce a second 'original' drawing. Three or four versions could be obtained in this manner without renewing the ink. The faintness of some of the lines in No. 135 suggest that this method may have been employed here. *Nos 6, 7, 12, 36, 37 and 135*

Rushbury, Sir Henry George, 1889–1968. Henry Rushbury was a distinguished draughtsman, watercolourist and etcher of architectural subjects. Born at Harborne, Birmingham, he studied at the Birmingham College of Art from 1903 to 1909. In 1912 he moved to London and was encouraged to take up etching and drypoint by Francis Dodd (1874–1949) and Muirhead Bone (1876–1953), two of the leading printmakers of the day. He was immediately successful. It was Rushbury's good fortune to find he had a natural talent for producing the kind of work which was selling well between the wars — black and white prints of architectural and topographical subjects. He became an acknowledged master of the 'line and wash' style of topographical draughtsmanship and was elected a member of the Royal Academy in 1936. He was an Official War Artist during both World Wars, became Keeper of the Royal Academy in 1949 and was knighted in 1964.

Sir Henry Rushbury was particularly interested in York and is known to have worked here during three periods of his career — in around 1933, in the 1940s and in 1965. York City Art Gallery has works from all three periods in the collection. *Nos 34, 66, 129, 136 and 137*

Southall, Joseph Edward, 1861–1944. Joseph Southall was a leading member of the Birmingham group of artist–craftsmen and a major figure in the tempera revival. He was born on 23 August 1861 in Nottingham of Quaker parents. On the death of his father in 1862 he and his mother went to live in Edgbaston, Birmingham, with his grandmother. He was educated at the Friends' School in Ackworth and later at Bootham School, York, where he was taught watercolour by the local artist Edwin Moore. After leaving school and until he became of age he was articled to a prominent firm of Birmingham architects, whilst in the evenings attending, from February to May 1879, a branch class of the Birmingham School of Art, and then, in the autumn of 1879, evening classes at the central School of Art, Birmingham. In 1883, while on holiday in Italy, he became an ardent admirer of the Italian Primitives and started to make a close examination of tempera paintings, an interest which was to lead to his being a co-founder of the Society of Painters in Tempera. Southall made several further trips to Italy and exhibited widely. He died on 6 November 1944 in Birmingham. *No. 60*

Storey, John, 1828–1888. John Storey was a topographical and architectural painter in watercolour, a lithographer and an illustrator. Born in Newcastle upon Tyne, he was educated by his father and was taught art by Thomas Miles Richardson the elder (1784–1848). During the 1850s, Storey evidently lived in York, forming an association with the lithographer William Bevan working in Judges' Court, Coney Street. This, however, was dissolved in 1859. His works were exhibited almost exclusively in Newcastle, the city where he was to spend most of his life. Storey died in Harrogate whilst attempting to recuperate from an illness. *Nos 9 and 26*

Tate, Edwin Ridsdale. See under Ridsdale Tate, Edwin.

Taylor, Edward, *c.* 1830–1908. Edward Taylor, architect, was probably born and brought up in York. He was certainly articled to the York architect George Fowler Jones and after qualifying went to London. On his return to York, he set up business first at 41 Parliament Street, then in Lendal, and finally at 7 Stonegate. From these addresses he received commissions ranging from Wesleyan chapels to domestic architecture. In 1866 his design for the temporary building to house the first Yorkshire Fine Art and Industrial Exhibition was erected in the field in front of Bootham Asylum. The exhibition was a great success and his building admired. A second Yorkshire Fine Art and Industrial Exhibition was planned and eventually took place in 1879; it was to be held in another specially erected building but this time one designed to have a permanent afterlife. Edward Taylor was again awarded the commission and this building, designed in the Italian Renaissance style and now housing the City Art Gallery, remains Taylor's best-known work. Taylor, who lived at the Sycamores, Bootham Terrace, died suddenly on 15 November 1908 at the age of seventy-seven. He was a prominent member of the Wesleyan Methodist church. *No. 84*

Tempest, Pierce, working 1670–died 1717. Pierce Tempest was a mezzotint and line engraver as well as being a printseller. He worked with Wenceslaus Hollar (1607–1677) and engraved portraits of the royal family. He is best known for this *Cries and Habits of London*, engraved on fifty plates after Marcellus Laroon (1653–1702) and published in 1688. He published a translation of Cesare Ripa's *Iconologia* in 1709, although he had stopped working as an engraver in 1705. He was buried at St Paul's, Covent Garden. *No. 91*

Thompson, James, working 1785. James Thompson was an etcher working around 1785 probably in London. That year his *Plan of the City of York and Ainsty* was produced. Nothing further is known about this engraver. *No. 10*

Toms, William Henry, died 1765. W. H. Toms was a London engraver of maps and topographical prints. He worked for antiquarians such as Sir William Stukely, for whom he made the engravings in *Itinerarium Curiosum*, published in 1724. Toms also worked for Francis Drake on *Eboracum*, 1736, signing some dozen plates, although a number of the unsigned plates could also be by him. Drake had to employ London engravers, as sufficiently skilled men were not available in York, at least not in the number required to produce the many prints planned for *Eboracum*. Toms continued to run a successful engraving business for the next thirty years, employing several apprentices, including John Boydell (1719–1804) who was to become the leading print publisher of his day and Lord Mayor of London. Toms's son Peter (died 1776) was also an artist: he became a well-known drapery painter who assisted many leading eighteenth-century portrait painters. *No. 118*

Varley, John, 1778–1842. John Varley is one of the best-known watercolour painters of the English school. He was born in Hackney on 17 August 1778 and was originally apprenticed to a silversmith. After his father's death in 1791 he was able to train as a painter and, when he was about fifteen, became a pupil of Joseph Charles Burrow, a topographical draughtsman and drawing-master. In the early 1800s Varley made a number of tours of Great Britain mainly in Wales and the North of England, visiting Yorkshire in 1803. The drawings he executed at the time were to be used again and again as source material, which to some extent explains the flagging imagination and more formalized approach adopted towards the end of his career. The work produced between 1805 and 1810 at the beginning of his career is generally considered his best. In 1804 Varley became a founder member of the Old Water-Colour Society. As well as being a fine watercolourist, Varley was an excellent teacher who strove to develop individual talent rather than to impose his own style. In this connection he issued a *Treatise on the Principles of Landscape Drawing* in eight parts between 1816 and 1821 and a *Pictorial Treatise on the Art of Drawing in Perspective and Precepts of Landscape Drawing* between 1815 and 1820. John Varley has been described as 'one of the most brilliant and attractive and also one of the most disappointing artists'. His works vary enormously in quality and his worth is made even more difficult to estimate by the fact that many watercolours attributed to him are in fact likely to be by pupils and imitators. He died in London. *Nos 67 and 68*

Varrall, John Charles, working 1818–1858. J. C. Varrall was a line engraver, who started working shortly before the demand for larger numbers of impressions encouraged engravers to use steel plates (which lasted longer than the copper ones previously employed). Little is known of his life, but his work can be seen in many books with topographical plates. *No. 132*

White, Francis, working 1770–1854. White was a surveyor of great accuracy. Nothing of his original work is known to survive. *No. 10*

White, Thomas, working *c.* 1800. Thomas White was a watercolour painter and drawing-master about whom very little is known. From the evidence of seven views in York City Art Gallery, it would seem that he was active in York around 1800 painting topographical views in a delicate style using a restrained colour scheme. The largest known group of works by this artist is in the Hailstone Collection, York Minster Library, which reveals that he also painted figures. *Nos 81 and 88*

Whittock, Nathaniel, working 1828–1858. Nathaniel Whittock was a draughtsman and lithographer who worked in Oxford and London during the second quarter of the nineteenth century. He styled himself 'Teacher of Drawing and Perspective and Lithographist to the University of Oxford'. *Nos 9 and 50*

Wild, Charles, 1781–1835. Charles Wild, an architectural draughtsman, was born in London in 1781 and was articled to Thomas Malton, the younger. He was elected a full member of the Old Water-Colour Society in 1812 and later became treasurer and secretary, but resigned in 1833 on account of his sight which had been growing progressively worse since 1827. His favourite subjects were cathedrals and colleges, which were almost always engraved. Most of his subjects were made in England but some also resulted from a tour of the Continent undertaken in the 1820s. Much of his work was published: his *Perspective Views of the Exterior and Interior Parts of the Metropolitan Church of York*, came out, in London, in 1809. His work is represented in many museums in England. *No. 94*

Topographical Index

Acknowledgements

The exhibition and publication would not have been possible without the help of many individuals: my grateful thanks are due to them all. The primary thanks must go to Ruth Prosser, until recently Conservator at York City Art Gallery, without whom this exhibition could not have taken place. Thereafter thanks on the technical side are due to David Richardson at Gillygate Framing, and to Terry Jones, technician, as well as to the team of attendants headed by John Stock.

Much of the information contained in the artists' biographies draws on research undertaken by previous members of Gallery staff: to John Ingamells, Norah Gillow, Michael Clarke, Janet Hughes and Tessa Sidey the real credit is due here. Research undertaken by Catharine James, from the College of Ripon and York St John has also been of great help in this connection. Additionally David Alexander has generously helped with a number of details but in particular the entry on Peter Chassereau.

My senior colleague, Richard Green, as well as writing the essay on York Artists and contributing to the biographies has also copy-edited the text, to which he has brought his unerring eye for inconsistences and flaws in logic. Helena Moore, former Exhibitions and Publicity Officer has given constant support, and an unstinting amount of practical advice. Helen Grundy, her successor has expertly handled the publicity, whilst Janet Moorby has speedily produced the typescript.

Graham Maney of Maney's Leeds, our printers, has been a source of patience, kindness and advice, whilst Chris Johnson-Green has been responsible for the elegant design of the maps, panels and labels.

Last but by no means least my heartfelt thanks go to Hugh Murray with whom it has been a great pleasure to work.

Sarah Riddick

Art Assistant, Organizer of the Exhibition,
and Co-ordinator of the Catalogue